Meeting Students Where They Live

Motivation in Urban Schools

Meeting Students Where They Live

Motivation in Urban Schools

Richard L. Curwin

ASCD

Alexandria, Virginia USA

ASCD®

1703 N. Beauregard St. • Alexandria, VA 22311-1714 USA
Phone: 800-933-2723 or 703-578-9600 • Fax: 703-575-5400
Web site: www.ascd.org • E-mail: member@ascd.org
Author guidelines: www.ascd.org/write

Gene R. Carter, *Executive Director;* Nancy Modrak, *Publisher;* Scott Willis, *Director, Book Acquisitions & Development;* Carolyn Pool, *Acquisitions Editor;* Julie Houtz, *Director, Book Editing & Production;* Miriam Goldstein, *Editor;* Catherine Guyer, *Senior Graphic Designer;* Mike Kalyan, *Production Manager;* Cynthia Stock, *Typesetter;* Carmen Yuhas, *Production Specialist*

All Web links in this book are correct as of the publication date below but may have become inactive or otherwise modified since that time. If you notice a deactivated or changed link, please e-mail books@ascd.org with the words "Link Update" in the subject line. In your message, please specify the Web link, the book title, and the page number on which the link appears.

PAPERBACK ISBN: 978-1-4166-0956-8   ASCD product #109110   n4/10
Also available as an e-book (see Books in Print for the ISBNs).

Quantity discounts for the paperback edition only: 10–49 copies, 10%; 50+ copies, 15%; for 1,000 or more copies, call 800-933-2723, ext. 5634, or 703-575-5634. For desk copies: member@ascd.org.

Library of Congress Cataloging-in-Publication Data

Curwin, Richard L., 1944-
   Meeting students where they live : motivation in urban schools / Richard L. Curwin.
     p. cm.
   Includes bibliographical references and index.
   ISBN 978-1-4166-0956-8 (pbk. : alk. paper) 1. Education, Urban—United States.
2. Community and school—United States. 3. Students with social disabilities—United States. 4. Public schools—Social aspects—United States. I. Title.
   LC5131.C87 2004
   371.009173'2—dc22
                               2009052798

20 19 18 17 16 15 14 13 12 11 10   1 2 3 4 5 6 7 8 9 10 11 12

This book is dedicated to
Nechama, Menashe, and Chana Koren
for their genuine hospitality to all, spiritual convictions,
and continual dedication to making life better for children.

Meeting Students Where They Live
Motivation in Urban Schools

Acknowledgments

The following people were instrumental in helping me write this book, and they have my gratitude for their support, suggestions, research, and accessibility:

Allen Mendler, David Curwin, Andrew Curwin, Danny (Menashe) Curwin, Maryln Appelbaum, Nancy Modrak, Carolyn Pool, Miriam Goldstein, Brian Mendler, Jon Crabbe, Ralph Amelan, Jessie Vance, Mark Phillips, Fisher Middle School, the Envision Schools of the Bay Area, my class at St. Joseph's University in Reading, Pennsylvania, Hillary Dames, the Milwaukee Public Schools, the Philadelphia Public School System, the New York City Public School System, the San Francisco Unified School District, Rick Smith, Dwight Allen, Sidney B. Simon, all those involved with Reclaiming Youth at Risk and the Black Hills seminars, Willeta Corbett, my patient pooch Daisy O'Grady, and all the wonderful schools, teachers, and students who invited me into their classrooms and shared their powerful stories and experiences with me.

A Teacher's Parable

There once was a king who wished for his son and sole heir to have a fine education. He sent servants out to post signs all over the kingdom advertising for a teacher for the prince. The signs indicated that if the king found the teacher fit for such a weighty responsibility, he would allow him to choose his own salary. Many people came from all over the kingdom to apply for the job. After testing all the applicants on the breadth and depth of their knowledge, the king narrowed his choice to three wise men.

He then asked each of the men how much they wanted to be paid and why they felt their services were worthy of that sum. The first man said that he should be paid 10,000 gold coins a month because he was the smartest man in all the land and could give the prince knowledge no one else had. He could reveal to him the secrets of the universe and the ideas of the world's greatest philosophers.

The second man said that he wanted 20,000 gold coins a month because he was the best teacher in all the land. He proclaimed that he could get anyone to learn anything. He spoke of how he could discipline a child to do anything he wanted; he was not afraid even of the prince.

The third man asked only for room and board and enough money to support his family. He said that he knew he was smart but not the smartest, and he knew he was a good teacher but not the best. He said that he should be chosen because it would be an honor to serve the king, the prince, and all the people of the land. He said that he wanted the next ruler of his beloved kingdom to be just as wise as his father.

The king, of course, chose the third man . . . and that is why teachers are paid such low salaries. All joking aside, this parable hopefully reminds us of what it means to be a teacher. To some people, teaching is a job and a paycheck; to others, it represents a place to exert power, a lofty platform from which to dispense knowledge. The finest teacher, however, realizes that he or she is in the classroom to help students achieve their full potential, in whatever form that may take.

Danny (Menashe) Curwin

Introduction

Many years ago, while living in San Francisco, I visited the home of a principal for whose school I was doing a long-term training program. She lived in a beautiful part of Maine. Standing in her backyard, as we looked out over a pristine lake and part of a lush mountain range, she said to me, "Now, you have to admit, this is more beautiful than San Francisco." I responded, "Your view is spectacular, I admit, but San Francisco is far more beautiful to me. When I look at your backyard, I see beautiful things, but in the city I see people—lots of different people—and to me, people are more beautiful than things."

I have heard it said that the "real" America exists in small towns, but for me, everything that is quintessentially American can be found in cities, from their diversity of people, language, food, and culture to their strength, resiliency, resourcefulness, and, yes, problems. If the fabled American melting pot exists anywhere, it is in our urban centers.

Some people might wonder why a book on motivating urban students is necessary, given the plethora of existing books on motivating students. Are the differences between urban youth and their suburban and rural counterparts really that significant? Certainly television, advertising, the Internet, music, and the proliferation of chain stores have had a homogenizing effect on children. Regardless of the environment in which they live, their style of dress, the way they talk, and the way they respond to a wide range of stimuli are all surprisingly similar.

Even with these similarities among students, the challenges teachers in urban environments face are unique and sometimes overwhelming in their scope. It may be cliché to say that people are both the city's greatest strength and its greatest curse, but when trying to educate urban youth, that observation feels anything but. The individuals that comprise any urban education system represent that system's greatest challenge and, simultaneously, the well from which we can draw the tools and resources to bring about change. Although most motivational strategies work with all students, urban youth have unique needs and circumstances that differentiate them from their suburban and rural counterparts.

Let's look at a small but important fragment of the school day: the time spent actually getting to school. In the suburbs and in rural areas, students might see, to varying degrees, houses, grass, animals, strip malls, cars, and foliage. Most of these students take school buses to school and spend the trip interacting with other students. In the city, students might see, at best, professionally attired men and women on their way to work, beautiful architecture, small specialty shops, and industrious laborers. At worst, students might see homeless men and women on the street, garbage, run-down buildings and stores, gridlocked traffic, and people who never make eye contact. Many urban students take public transportation to school rather than a school bus—a very different experience indeed.

Thus, before urban students even get to school, their experience already differs greatly from that of students in the suburbs or the country. Their physical and emotional reactions and worldview are all inescapably informed by their environment, all of which affects their readiness to learn, appreciation for authority, trust of strangers, and disposition toward feeling hopeful about the future.

Janet Milanowski, a teacher from Adelante High School in Grand Rapids, Michigan, notes that urban teachers face myriad problems that other teachers either do not face or face far less often. These include poverty, various degrees of English proficiency, minimal parental involvement, and a high rate of teen pregnancy. Nicole Dood, an elementary teacher from the same district, says that on any given day she must be a teacher, parent, social worker, counselor, nurse, and therapist.

When working with hearing-impaired students, speaking to the class while simultaneously writing on the chalkboard is useless. Students must be able to see the teacher's face while she talks. Facing students and speaking directly to them is also helpful in regular education classes, but for hearing-impaired students, it is essential. Similarly, most, if not all, strategies that make learning more accessible for urban students can be used successfully with all students. The difference is that for urban students, they are critically important. The strategies I present in this book, therefore, will work for all students in need of motivating, but they are designed with the specific challenges and needs of urban students in mind.

In June of 2008, *Sports Illustrated* published the article "How Dreams Die," which described in detail how sports have been unable to save student athletes from gang violence in Oakland and Richmond, California. Eighteen-year-old Terrance Kelly, a well-known local football star, was killed in a gang-related shooting before he could attend the college that had offered him a scholarship. Many in Kelly's neighborhood spoke of the hopelessness of their lives, believing that if star athletes could not get out of the "hood," then what chance did they have? I wonder how many other urban youths feel the same way. How can students be motivated to learn in an atmosphere of hopelessness, violence, and fear?

When I was in graduate school in the early 1970s at the University of Massachusetts, the dean of the School of Education and one of the most important educators of our time, Dwight Allen, set up a unique program to improve urban education. Several doctoral students and faculty members flew from Amherst to Brooklyn, New York, where we offered courses and training to paraprofessionals so that they could be certified to become teachers. Most of the participants were middle-aged women, mostly minorities, from Brooklyn. Their love of children and their desire to teach were unparalleled. I saw a commitment to and compassion for neighborhood children that stirred in me a lifelong desire to change the urban academic landscape as part of my professional responsibility.

Dreams for a better future can counterbalance the hopelessness that poverty, poor facilities, and violence instill in students. During the 1990s, high school students in the Mission District in San Francisco were involved in a unique program. After school, they were brought to fast-food restaurants, gas stations, and warehouses, not to see burgers getting flipped or gas being pumped, but to meet the managers and owners. They got to meet people making just as much money as drug dealers and pimps and driving the same fancy cars, but living without the fear of prison or death. They learned that financial security can coexist with safety and that hope comes from studying, not crime.

When I sat down to begin writing this book, I realized that it is impossible to write about making things better without commenting first on what is wrong. Because this book is about urban problems and because most urban populations are composed disproportionately of minorities, I feared that the book might inadvertently imply that minorities are a problem. I hope that no reader mistakenly walks away with that impression.

I had similar fears when I gave a talk to an all-female, African American audience in Oakland, California. As I began my presentation on improving parenting skills, I apologized to my audience for being different ethnically and culturally, hoping to bridge the racial divide in a gentle, inviting way. One woman stood up and said, "We know you're white. We don't care. Just help us be better moms. We love our children and you may know something good." The audience applauded, and my anxiety slipped away.

As you progress through this book, you will notice frequent references to "effort." Although it might seem repetitive or even begin to satiate—you will learn that term in Chapter 2—its consistent (and persistent) appearance is not without design or intent. Effort applies in every chapter and relates to every strategy because effort is the key factor in creating motivation.

Motivation grows out of hope. This book seeks to offer practical suggestions for eliminating the school and classroom factors that squelch hope and for building on those that allow it to flourish and grow.

1

The Difficulty of Motivating Urban Youth

The word *motivation,* as used in this book, refers to *wanting* to learn as opposed to *having* to learn. I pay my bills not because I *want* to but because I *have* to in order to avoid the consequences of not paying them. Thus, by my definition, I am not motivated to pay them. Similarly, when students do their work under the threat of unpleasant consequences, they are not motivated.

If sufficiently feared, threats can produce behavior changes, but students who are continually threatened often develop a psychological "immune system" that can render such attempts at coercion useless. These students have been threatened so many times that they no longer fear the worst a teacher can inflict upon them. Ironically, when threats do work, it is usually with good students, who rarely receive them and, consequently, are more frightened by them. Regardless, changes in behavior do not necessarily equal motivation.

I observed a teacher in Philadelphia who continually used threats—ranging from serving detention to making calls home—to get her students to do their work. Many of her students exerted just enough effort to get by, doing minimal work with minimal results. In my conferences with this teacher, I focused mainly on two strategies: reducing the use of threats and introducing joy into the classroom. The students who hadn't been doing any work didn't respond to the changes in the classroom (they became our next project), but those who had been doing some work, albeit the bare minimum, did far more and vastly improved work.

Fair Trumps Equal

A friend of mine once said that covering material is not great teaching; uncovering it is. And the techniques we use to uncover material for students can greatly affect their motivation to learn. What is motivating to one student is not necessarily motivating to all. Some students like group activities; others hate them. Some learn by listening, others by seeing, and still others by doing. These factors all affect motivation. To successfully motivate, we must accept that fair is not the same as equal—that is, applying the same motivational strategy to all students may be equal, but if one student responds well to that technique and another student does not, it is almost certainly not fair. IEPs (individualized education plans) operate on this principle, as does individualized instruction. The same is true for motivational strategies: they work best when individualized.

José and Ike were two 5th grade students who refused to do any homework. When he got home from school, José was expected to help his father in his family's bodega until 7 p.m. By the time he finished working in the store, he was too tired to do his homework. Ike's problem was more severe. He lived in a middle-class section of town with what appeared to be attentive parents. A home visit, however, quickly revealed why he didn't do his homework. His living room had a large, deep hole in the floor filled with pizza boxes, beer cans, other trash, and rats. Ike was too afraid of the rats—he even slept with a baseball bat on his lap—to concentrate on his work.

Both of these students had the same problem, but the solution to that problem was, by necessity, very different for each boy. Ike's case was turned over to social services. The hole in his living room was eventually filled and the rats exterminated. Not surprisingly, his work gradually began to come in when due. Meanwhile, José's father agreed to set aside time to let his son do his homework before expecting him to help in the store and even found a little time to sit with him while he did it. Responding only to the behavioral symptom in these cases (i.e., not doing homework) rather than addressing the root causes of the symptom and applying the appropriate solutions to those causes would have solved nothing in these situations.

Measuring Motivation

Motivation cannot be inferred by measuring achievement. One student who tries his hardest may get 50 percent on a test, while another student who does not try at all could get 95 percent on the same test. The true determiner of motivation is effort. In fact, the goal of motivation is to increase effort. Although effort alone will not increase achievement, achievement can be seen as a by-product of effort. When students do not try, they are not producing at their highest potential. Conversely, when students put in high levels of effort, achievement does tend to increase overall. Assessment of learning works best when it accounts for this variable.

Of course, to be truly effective, students must use best practices as well as put in effort. Trying hard incorrectly leads to little improvement. Thus, we have the learning cycle: using motivational strategies, the teacher shows students the right way to learn necessary skills, and the students try hard to master those skills. Sounds perfect, and it is when it works; but is it ever that easy?

Motivating Urban Youth

Urban schools, like all other schools, have some students who are highly motivated, some who are occasionally motivated, and some who care very little, if at all, about learning. Plenty of urban schools are effective and do not struggle with the problems discussed here. If the discussion here seems overly negative, it is because I am focusing on improving learning for those students who have chosen not to try, and the reasons behind that choice are almost never positive. I am not blind to the excellence exhibited by so many teachers, administrators, schools, programs, and parents. Nor do I feel hopeless, negative, or discouraged about urban youth. In fact, the suggestions I offer for improving motivation among urban students center around hope and moving away from a system that equates "increasing motivation" with either punishment or bribery. But aiming for a more hopeful, improved future requires acknowledging and understanding the present situation, namely that many urban schools do face a constellation of serious problems. The following seven plagues present the greatest challenge to urban schools and their students.

Racism

Racism has various debilitating effects: it sows students' mistrust of teachers, contributes to teachers' negative characterizations of students of certain races, and leads to student conflicts, even fights. Minority students are especially vulnerable to the phenomenon known as the "school-to-prison pipeline."

Here's how it works. Minority students—many of whom already have limited access to educational opportunities—tend to receive harsher school punishments for their infractions than nonminority students do. Such punishments may include suspension and expulsion, which further isolate students from academic instruction. In a nutshell, when schools fail to educate students and mete out extreme punishments for minor offenses, they limit students' future opportunity and move them toward the prison system (Brown, 2003; Ferguson, 2000; Gordon, Della Piana, & Keleher, 2001a, 2001b; Johnson, Boyden, & Pittz, 2001; Losen & Edley, 2001; Skiba & Leone, 2001; Skiba, Michael, Nardo, & Peterson, 2002; Vavrus & Cole, 2002; Wald & Losen, 2004a, 2004b).

When I was in high school, my best friend Bob and I hung out at Fenway Park every day after school during baseball season. Over time, we got to know many players from visiting teams, mostly African American players who were, by and large, more receptive to us than their white teammates. Some of these players eventually befriended us and came to our homes for dinners, played stickball with us, and allowed us to record interviews with them. In these interviews, the players told us how different and difficult life was for black players. Because of my friendship with these men, I developed a sensitivity to racism unusual for white kids of that era. In college, I worked within the black community to recruit more minority students (and not just athletes). Most of my friends were black, and I sported an Afro that my friends said was a waste on a white man. I also engaged in blockbusting—buying a house in an all-white neighborhood with some friends and then turning it over to a black family. And I've dedicated much of my professional career to finding ways for minorities to get quality education.

Given my history, you can imagine how surprised I was when two black administrators complained to seminar organizers that I was racist after I privately asked them why they were late to a session, disturbing the other participants with an unruly entrance. Their accusation hurt my feelings, but I tried not to take it personally, knowing that it was likely based on assumptions solidified by their own life experiences. My suggestion for teachers accused of racism, no matter their background or race, is to try not to become defensive. Instead, ask accusers how you can meet their needs without offending them. As difficult as it may be, try to find common ground. Here are two possible ways to begin the conversation, one directed toward a student, the other toward a parent:

• Teacher to student: "I'm sorry you were hurt by what I did/said. Can you tell me a better way to ask you to be quiet when I need your attention that won't offend you?"

• Teacher to parent: "I'm sure in your past you have felt disrespected due to your race. I never want to do that with you or your child. Can you help me find a way to stop your child from hitting other kids without disrespecting him?"

Tower of Babel

Among most urban school populations, at least two languages are spoken. In some schools, that number is much higher. It is difficult enough at times to teach native English speakers, let alone students with a poor grasp of your first language. Unfortunately, funding and other support systems have not caught up with the reality of multilingual student populations. Check (2006) observes that "dealing with multiple languages in urban schools is underfunded and . . . a lot of work still needs to be done." Here are some ways to alleviate the challenges:

• Have paraprofessionals with multiple language skills come into your classroom to help translate.

• Invite community members, especially retired or elderly people, into your classroom to act as interpreters.

• Ask students who are more fluent in English to translate what you are saying to less fluent students and to help you understand those students.

- Ask teachers who speak the secondary language to help you prepare written assignments and tests.
- Seek out older students with free periods or those serving in-school suspension (see page 77) to act as interpreters.

Even among native English speakers, language barriers exist. A serious and frequently ignored discrepancy exists between the vocabularies of middle-class white students and poor African American students upon entering school. Samuel Betances, author of *Ten Steps to the Head of the Class*, estimates that the latter know about one-third of the number of words that the former know by school age. Based on this discrepancy, we make negative assumptions about minority children's ability to read, write, and comprehend, when in fact they just have a smaller initial vocabulary (Betances, 1998). Such assumptions can lead to false conclusions and labels that negatively affect minority children throughout their school careers.

Drugs

Obviously, drug use and abuse are not limited to urban schools. Data from the National Longitudinal Study of Adolescent Health, one of the most comprehensive and rigorous studies of the behavior of American high school students, tell us that suburban public high school students have sex, drink, smoke, use illegal drugs, and engage in delinquent behavior just as often as urban public high school students do (Greene & Forster, 2004). But certainly teachers and administrators in urban areas must find ways to deal with drug use and distribution in their schools. Students can be involved with drugs in all kinds of ways. For example, they may

- Use in school.
- Use at home but not in school.
- Use at home and come to school high.
- Sell or distribute in school.
- Enable drug use by not reporting their friends who do any of the above because there is such a strong code against informing.
- Have parents who use at home.

All these ways of being involved with drugs affect students. Drug use, whether by students or by their friends or family,

- Compromises students' ability to learn.
- Connects students to other drug users.
- Places students in danger of incarceration.
- Compromises their home life (especially if family members use drugs).

If legal issues are involved, such as drug use and dealing at school, the police must be called in. Make it clear from the beginning that you will inform the authorities if you see students breaking the law. Tell students not to reveal anything to you that you might need to report, because you will not hesitate to do so. If a student's behavior leads you to suspect him or her of drug use or distribution, voice your suspicions and the basis for them. Listen to the student's answers, but clearly state your legal obligations and what you will do next if the behavior continues.

If you know that drug use is preventing parents from meeting their responsibilities, talk with your administrator about informing the parents of your concerns. In some cases, this may not be the best option and the school may need to call social services.

If students come to class high, address the students' behavior rather than the cause. This may seem contradictory to what I've argued previously, but in the case of drug use, our influence does not extend beyond the school boundaries. Addressing the underlying reasons for students' drug use is beyond the scope of our abilities. In this book, however, I suggest techniques that a teacher can use to deal with specific behavior. For example, if the student does not participate in class, use the Terminator technique discussed in Chapter 2. If the student doesn't complete his or her homework, try the strategies offered in Chapter 10.

Of course, some educators have used drugs themselves, and teachers frequently ask me, "What do I say when a student asks me if I've ever tried drugs? I want to be honest, but I don't want to legitimize drug use." My answer is (1) don't come to school high, and (2) ask the student if he can keep a secret. If he says "Yes," then tell him "So can I."

Perhaps the most abused drug among teens is alcohol. According to the Web site Learn-About-Alcoholism.com, alcohol is the top drug of choice for children and adolescents. Each day, 7,000 children in the United States under the age of 16 take their first drink. In addition, more than 35 percent of adults with an alcohol problem developed symptoms by age 19. Overall, more than 100,000 U.S. deaths are caused by excessive alcohol consumption each year. Clearly, something must be done to stem the tide of student drinking at an early age. This requires a joint effort between parents and schools. We need education programs for parents, agreements among all groups (including parents and educators) to provide more diligent supervision, and increased communication among community groups, parents, and schools.

Gangs

According to Laub and Lauritsen, "the presence of street gangs at school can be very disruptive to the school environment because they may not only create fear among students but also increase the level of violence in school" (1998). In the National Center for Education Statistics' *Indicators of School Crime and Safety* (DeVoe et al., 2004), 21 percent of students surveyed reported that there were gangs at their schools. Of all the students surveyed, "students in urban schools were the most likely to report the presence of street gangs at their school (31 percent), followed by suburban students and rural students, who were the least likely to do so (18 and 12 percent, respectively)." The report goes on to note, however, that "no difference was detected between 2001 and 2003 in percentages of students who reported the presence of street gangs, regardless of school location."

Students join gangs for a variety of reasons: for excitement, protection, friendship, family affiliations, neighborhood recruitment, or the support and stability that they aren't getting at home. Students often view gang members as glamorous and powerful, a perception that is difficult to combat. As with drug abuse, our ability as educators to change students' gang behavior is limited. We can, however, take a strong stand against gang behavior in school and try to steer that behavior toward more positive outcomes.

Students should not be permitted to wear gang colors, insignia, or paraphernalia in school. Admittedly, it is difficult to stop this when "showing colors" can be something as subtle as unbuttoning a specific button on a shirt or wearing a collar in a certain way. Nonetheless, we must be vigilant about observing the codes students use to signify gang affiliation.

In addition, schools must develop a system that allows students and faculty to anonymously report gang activity in schools, including drug distribution, fighting, and intimidation. This will require facing our fears about our own safety. Acting alone is never a good idea when dealing with gang activity. Most cities have a gang task force. Be sure that your school works closely with one if you have a gang problem.

Some curricular content areas may offer opportunities to introduce the topic of gangs—for example, social studies, art, music, and composition. Consider taking advantage of these in-class opportunities to discuss the issue in your school. Invite former gang members who have successfully gotten out to speak to your classes. Their firsthand experiences may bring home to kids that it is better not to join in the first place than to try to get out later. Coordinate community services where available to find alternative activities for students, such as sports, clubs, community improvement programs, and volunteer work.

Violence

Violence in schools typically manifests itself in one of four ways: physically, emotionally, sexually, or as destruction or theft of property. The behaviors that fall within these categories range from name-calling and sexual taunts to fighting and carrying weapons onto school property. Some of these behaviors (e.g., carrying weapons into school or getting into physical altercations) are obviously dangerous and disruptive to the learning process, but what about less egregious behavior? Where should school administrators draw the line between behavior that lacks ill intent but may nonetheless be considered problematic? For example, is giving a welcoming shoulder tap the same as hitting? Are middle school students who playfully shove one another fighting? Does asking a girl out on a date after she denied the first request constitute sexual harassment? In an attempt to eliminate confusion, some schools have made *all* touching, even handshakes, a suspendable offense. Although understandable, such a blanket response is not realistic. Each school must define reasonable behavior boundaries given the age of its students, prevailing school culture, and potential for escalation. One possible approach is to involve a range of school representatives—staff, administrators, parents, and students—in developing acceptable behavioral boundary lines and a range of consequences for crossing those lines. I discuss these ideas further in Chapter 3.

However we choose to respond to school violence, we must respond. In a 2003 survey of high school students, 17.1 percent reported having carried a weapon to school during the 30 days preceding the survey (Grunbaum et al., 2004). In response to a 2000 survey on crime and safety, 71 percent of the public elementary and secondary schools surveyed indicated that they had experienced at least one violent incident during the 1999–2000 school year (Larsen, 2003). Many students who display violent or abusive behavior are themselves exposed to such behavior outside school and are in need of mental health services. Frequently, the only such services available to these children are those provided through the school (Stein et al., 2003). This lays a great deal of responsibility at the feet of educators, because statistics clearly indicate the long-reaching effects of school violence: children who engage in bullying are more likely to become adult criminals (Taub, 2002) and eventually pass on the concept that violence is acceptable to their own children.

Lack of Family Structure and Stability

A supportive and stable home environment plays a defining role in how moti-vated students are to learn. Certainly, not all urban children come from abusive or dysfunctional families. In fact, the National Center for Education Statistics (Lippman, Burns, & McArthur, 1996) reports that "urban students were equally or more likely than other students to have families with certain characteristics that have been found to support desirable education outcomes, including high parental educational attainment, high expectations for their children's educa-tion, and frequent communication about school." This same study, however, found that many urban children were less likely to have other fundamental supports, including "the family structure, economic security, and stability that are most associated with desirable educational outcomes."

Often, school officials view parents or other adults in the home as an impedi-ment to students' motivation and achievement, perceiving them as adversar-ies instead of supporters of their children's education. These officials blame different cultural values and a lack of family structure for poor academic achievement. Parents, not surprisingly, frequently see school officials as the problem, accusing them of discrimination and insensitivity (Atkinson & Juntunen, 1994). We must endeavor to remove this wall between educators and parents.

We do not have the power to change our students' family lives, but we do have the power to give them a welcoming, supportive, and safe school environment. School is often the safest place, both emotionally and physically, in many students' lives. We also have an obligation to build the best possible relationships with parents and other significant adults in our students' lives. This book offers suggestions on how to do both of these things. Finally, we have the responsibility to contact social services if we perceive that a student's family life is endangering him. Although this is a drastic step, to be undertaken with great caution, it is sometimes necessary.

I was a behavior consultant for Lipman Hall, a lockdown facility for teenage male sex offenders in Newark, New Jersey, that closed in June 2004. It held 220 students/inmates at the time I was helping them. All 220 of the teenagers housed there had been sexually abused themselves. Their parents or the adults in their homes did most of the molesting. I saw firsthand how children pay for the sins of a poor family life or, in these cases, a toxic one.

When assigned to the facility, each student was offered a teddy bear if he wanted one. Monica Crapis, the principal at the time, told me that every student took one, and most slept with theirs. The juxtaposition of hardened sexual criminals sleeping with teddy bears in a lockdown facility is a powerful image of how severely damaging a destructive family can be.

High Dropout Rates

In far too many cases, the streets are more attractive to students than our city schools are. Fourteen urban school districts, including Detroit, Baltimore, New York, Milwaukee, Cleveland, Los Angeles, Miami, Dallas, Denver, and Houston, have on-time graduation rates below 50 percent (Toppo, 2006). And when students drop out of school, for whatever reason, incarceration is often their next stop. As Harlow (2003) observes, "school dropouts are vulnerable to incarceration regardless of race. In 1997, almost 75 percent of state inmates lacked a high school diploma." African American male dropouts, however, are significantly more vulnerable than white male dropouts are. Harlow (2003) further notes that "by the time high school dropouts reach age 34, 12 percent of white men and 52 percent of black men have prison records." In 1999, 7.2 percent of young white high school dropouts were in prison, compared with 41.2 percent of young African American high school dropouts (Western, Pettit, & Guetzkow, 2002).

This outcome has become so prevalent that many urban students seem resigned to it or, even more alarmingly, see it as a goal. During a discussion with students at an urban middle school in San Jose, California, I asked, "What do you want to do when you graduate from high school?" Many of them responded, "Go to prison." When I asked them why, their answers ranged from "It's cool" to "You get respect in this neighborhood [when you go to prison]" to "So I can see my dad." As evidenced by these students' answers, urban settings often foster a culture of accepting and even honoring failure, a mind-set that particularly flourishes among the least motivated. Even worse, it begins to affect those students who *are* motivated to learn. Students who do well are castigated and rejected by many of their peers. I asked Henry, a high school student from San Francisco's Hunters Point neighborhood, why a bright young man like himself was doing so poorly in school. His response? "So I can have friends."

Sometimes, students' concerns are far more basic than worrying about social acceptance. When a student's home life is truly toxic—filled with drug and alcohol addiction, physical abuse, neglect, dangerous or unsanitary living conditions, family members in gangs or prison, and the responsibility for raising younger siblings or taking care of parents—just getting to school, let alone graduating, can present a challenge. Teachers do not always know what happens at home or understand its effect on school behavior.

I recall a 7th grade boy who came to school disheveled, dirty, and wearing the same clothes day after day. The other students complained about his smell. The teacher wanted to send him home until he practiced good hygiene. A home visit soon showed why this was the worst possible solution. His mother was an alcoholic who left this boy and his younger sister locked in the backyard when she left home to go on drinking binges. The kids had no water, clean clothes, or food. They had to forage to eat and were forced to sleep on a pile of dirt. They were informed that if they told anyone, they would "pay the price." Sending them back to the yard was certainly the wrong solution. The school called social services immediately, and the situation improved. Like Ike, the young man mentioned at the beginning of this chapter, students may be contending with a home environment that doesn't meet even the most fundamental needs of shelter and safety. In such cases, a teacher's best efforts to provide a positive, supportive environment away from the home are simply not enough.

Setting aside the family situations over which we have no control, we must do a better job of keeping children in school. Fortunately, despite the many challenges discussed so far, the options for doing so are plentiful. Alternative schools have proven effective at keeping kids engaged in learning and off the streets. Most of the alternative schools I have visited are filled with dedicated staff members who actually prefer to teach troubled youth and who provide an atmosphere that fairly shouts, "All are welcome here!" These schools may employ varied structures, strategies, and policies, but they all offer hope to their students. Most students refuse to return to regular school even if offered the opportunity.

Charter schools offer another avenue for keeping students in school. As with alternative schools, I have personally observed the dedication of the teachers and administrators who staff these schools. The Envision Schools, a group of charter schools in California's San Francisco Bay Area, are perfect examples of what schools have the capacity to be: student-centered, with individualized instruction, high but reachable standards, and a committed staff that has built each school into a genuine community.

This book offers suggestions that every school can use to keep its students in the classroom. Chapter 6 (Welcoming All Students to School and Class) is especially relevant. Motivating and encouraging students who do not want to learn begins with five key changes in attitude:

- Build hope.
- Believe in students.
- Genuinely care about students.
- Refuse to give up on students, no matter how hard they try to make us quit.
- Stop thinking "What difference can I make?" and start making a difference. Teachers have the power to change lives. Teachers changed mine, and there's a good chance a teacher changed yours.

Changes in attitude, however, are not enough. We must also take action. Concrete steps we can take include

- Welcoming all students.
- Building lessons that involve and engage.
- Motivating and energizing ourselves.
- Using evaluation to encourage and build learning rather than defeat it.

Teaching from a Center of Love

When we teach urban youth, we can teach from a center of fear, or we can teach from a center of love. When we operate from a center of fear, we pursue self-protection. We promote values and practices that focus on control, uniformity, and lack of tolerance. When we teach from a center of love, we engage in pursuing what is best for students. We promote values and practices that focus on compassion, understanding, tolerance, and safety for all.

The remainder of this book focuses on specific values and practices that can help educators make the above changes in attitude and action a reality.

2

Ten Quick Strategies to Increase Motivation

Sometimes small, quick strategies can make major differences in student motivation. They can increase student involvement with the lesson and stop interference and distractions. Each of the following strategies was developed to meet the needs of urban students and has had great results.

Follow Through

Tenth grade history teacher Ms. Edison saw Eunice talking on her cell phone during class. She quietly approached Eunice and respectfully asked her to put the phone away. Then she walked back to the front of the classroom and resumed her lesson. Eunice never put her phone away. Down the hall, Ms. Rosenberg told her class to quiet down several times, but started teaching before her students complied. In both cases, the teachers failed to follow through. Ms. Edison should have stayed with Eunice, gradually moving closer and repeating, "I need that cell put away now," until Eunice complied. Only then should she have returned to the lesson. Similarly, Ms. Rosenberg needed to wait for the class to quiet down before starting her lesson.

It helps students who have highly unstructured home lives, as is the case for so many urban youth, to understand that your requests are serious and that you will follow through on them. This reinforces the underlying stability of the classroom environment, reduces power struggles, and, hopefully, cuts down on the kind of repetitive requests for behavior changes that students inevitably come to view as nagging and that, as a result of this perception, frequently erode motivation.

Let All Students Hear

Many urban classrooms have more students than any one person can effectively teach. Students sometimes have difficulty hearing the teacher and one another regardless of class size, but this problem intensifies in an overly large class, either because the space itself is bigger or because the buzz of conversation makes listening impossible. Students rarely tell their teacher when they cannot hear the lesson or another student's comments. Instead, they simply tune out. If you have ever been in a workshop or similar group where you had to struggle to hear the questions being asked, then you understand the frustration these students feel. Solve the problem by privately asking students on the sides and in the back of the room if they can hear you. It might seem repetitious, but do this at least twice a week. In addition, when students interact with you during a discussion or question-and-answer session, repeat for the class the answers given or comments made. Keep in mind that although you can hear them, other students might not.

Stop Student Texting

We cannot escape the degree to which cell phones and texting are ensconced in our culture. The Pew Internet & American Life Project reported in 2009 that 71 percent of American teens own a cell phone (compared with 45 percent in 2004), 50 percent sometimes use informal capitalization and punctuation in school assignments, and 38 percent have used texting lingo in schoolwork (Lenhart, 2009). Not only do students text one another throughout the day, but parents also frequently text students, usually for no good reason. (Have you ever asked a student to put his cell phone away only to have him say, "But it's my mother. . . ."?) Taking cell phones away may not be worth the battle it usually generates or the loss of learning caused by that battle. In addition, cell phones can save lives in emergencies. I prefer holding a class meeting to discuss how to handle inappropriate cell phone use. Solicit students' suggestions and use them when you discover inappropriate cell phone use.

Of course, stopping cell phone use in class requires us to detect it, a challenge in itself. Students find ways to text on devices hidden in pockets, earpieces can easily be hidden by long hair, and adults can't always hear high-pitched ring tones. Seeing cell phone use from the front of the classroom is difficult, so make sure you move around the room as you teach (a technique that can help address a variety of problems). If you see a student using a cell phone or other mobile device, be firm and insistent about putting it away. (See the Terminator strategy in the following section.) Use the plan adopted in your class meeting. If a student consistently receives calls or texts from a parent during class time, call the parent—or ask an administrator to call—and politely insist that he or she contact the school office rather than interrupt class.

A teacher from Dallas found a creative way to address the cell phone problem. If students wanted to bring a cell phone to class, they had to pay a dollar at the beginning of the year (help was provided for students who couldn't pay). The teacher took a dime from the dollar every time a student refused to put his phone away when asked. If a student's dollar ran out, he or she had to pay another. The money collected was donated to a charity chosen by the class at the end of the year, and the unused balance was returned to the students.

Be Persistent (aka The Terminator)

Sometimes when we call on a student who is uninvolved or not paying attention, he shrugs his shoulders or looks away. "I don't know," he says, his tone of voice proclaiming "And I don't care, either." We may be tempted to give up and call on a student who is more likely to respond. We all prefer to call on students who are actively involved. Rather than let this student go, however, it makes more sense to show him that you expect him to be involved in classroom activities. One response is to channel Arnold Schwarzenegger's iconic character the Terminator, whose tag line was "I'll be back." The following sample dialogue demonstrates the Terminator technique:

Teacher: Darleen, what is the definition of an adjective?

Darleen: I dunno.

Teacher: That's OK. I don't expect you to know everything. But you deserve another chance. I'll call on you again soon.

Darleen: Whatever!

Teacher (seven minutes later): Darleen, here's another chance for you. What is the definition of a noun?

Darleen: Still dunno.

Teacher: That's OK, but you still deserve a chance to get one right. I'll call on you again soon.

(The teacher continues to call on Darleen until she gives an answer.)

The idea is to let your student know that you won't let her off the hook and that you expect her to answer. This works best with gentle persistence. In other words, call on the student enough to show resolve but not so much as to be overbearing or aggressive. Each student has a different tolerance for persistence, so watch for signs of severe frustration. Naturally, the student will show some frustration when continually called on, but no student can be allowed to believe that she can simply coast through class. This only reinforces the student's self-perception that she is unable to learn.

Reduce Distractions

All students can get distracted, but children with ADHD (attention-deficit hyperactivity disorder) are especially susceptible to interruptions and distractions. Maryln Appelbaum, noted author and teacher trainer, suggests screening out visual distractions by building a carrel desk out of two manila folders stapled together to form a three-sided structure. In addition, due to their tendency to fidget, students with ADHD sometimes create distractions for other students. One such behavior is pencil tapping. The problem is not the tapping but the resulting noise. Letting the student tap on tissue, a sponge, or a mouse pad eliminates the distraction while still allowing the student to expend pent-up energy.

To accommodate students who find it difficult to sit through an entire class period, consider providing stand-up desks or asking the music department to loan out music stands. Richards (2008) points out that "stand-up desks provide a firm footing for fidgety students and teachers report improved focus and behavior." The ability to stand up or sit down as needed during a lesson provides movement and comfort for those students who simply cannot sit still. This option can be offered to students of all ages, but it is especially useful for those in middle school. Don't forget the "fair is not necessarily equal" principle discussed in Chapter 1 when students who do not need this accommodation ask for it.

Start On Time

Many teachers, especially at the secondary level, don't start class on time. Some are still preparing the day's lesson, some are writing the lesson on the board, and still others are simply waiting for all their students to arrive. Starting class late, however, can exacerbate tardiness: the later class starts, the later students know they can be. Starting on time is important because, like many of the other suggestions and techniques I offer in this book, it provides a predictable environment for students who have unstructured home lives. To avoid starting late, make sure you are prepared to start class the minute you enter the classroom. In addition, use overheads or flip charts rather than spending time writing on the chalkboard. Lastly, do not wait for tardy students. Students who show up on time shouldn't have to wait for those who don't. The best strategy to combat tardiness is to start class with something students do not want to miss (see Chapter 7 for suggestions on how to do this). I do not believe in removing tardy students from class or restricting their entry, but if they are late, then make it clear that they are missing something.

Greet Students at the Door

At least two or three times a week, be at the door when students enter the classroom. Greet as many as you can with a personal statement, making sure to include your least motivated students. For some urban students, your greeting may be the most positive one-on-one interaction they get all day. The following are examples of simple statements you can make to welcome your students and start the class on a positive note:

- "Pedro, I'm glad you're on time. I miss you when you're late."
- "Wilma, let's have a great class today, OK?"
- "Sara, I have a special question I reserved especially for you to answer today. I hope you like it."

Protect Against Procedural Satiation

Satiation, in this context, refers to the process of losing power over time. Most procedures satiate. If you have a technique to quiet the class, it stops working after a while. When I taught 7th grade, I stood quietly in front of my class and waited for quiet. At first it worked, just as my college professors said it would. After two weeks, however, I could have stood at the front of the class for 100 years and no one would have noticed. Develop between 5 and 10 "get quiet" procedures and switch when one stops working. Here are some ideas to start you off:

- Raise your hand. Everyone who sees this raises his or her hand and stops talking.
- Ask everyone to say "Shush."
- Form groups. Assign one student to be the group's "shusher" for the week. Ask the shushers to shush their group.
- Play a flute, recorder, or some other soothing instrument. In a particularly noisy class, a drum or trombone might be more effective.
- Sing a certain song and have the students sing along with you.

Other common classroom routines for which you will likely need a variety of procedures include lining up, handing in homework, and leaving class for the bathroom, a snack, or naptime.

Follow Your Own Rules

Children are bombarded by examples of adults who say one thing and do another. In inner-city environments, this is especially true. How can messages to stay away from gangs and drugs be effective, for example, with so many gangs and drug houses in plain view? These children are confronted by parents who demand the truth but lie themselves, shopkeepers who rail against stealing but overcharge for necessary items, and adult conduct that contradicts the behaviors lauded in the home, school, and place of worship. Children need role models whose actions correspond to their words. If you tell your students you expect them to arrive on time, then be on time yourself. If you expect your students to turn in work on time, then return grades and comments to them on time. If you want students to dress appropriately, then do so yourself. Failing to follow your own rules places you in the category of yet another "do as I say, not as I do" adult. In addition, when students see teachers breaking their own rules, it sends a message that the rule is unimportant and that it is OK for them to break the rules, too.

Encourage Student Humor

A number of comedians from urban backgrounds—Bill Cosby, Lewis Black, Eddie Murphy, and Chris Rock among them—tell stories about having their personalities stifled by teachers who were uncomfortable with their jokes and humorous antics. Trying to suppress such behavior usually results in a power struggle in which no one wins. Instead, consider turning your classroom comedians' talents into another tool for motivating students. In order to achieve this, it may be necessary to teach students the difference between appropriate and inappropriate language and content. Here are five ways to encourage your students' use of humor and include it in the classroom in a productive way:

• Ask the class clown to come prepared to tell one or two jokes in class. Have the student tell the joke(s) during transitions between activities.

• Ask two or three students to be ready to start class with a quick joke two or three times a week.

• Break students into small groups of three to four students and have them come up with funny sayings about what you are about to teach. For example, a 4th grader came up with this limerick before a science lesson on frogs:

There was a frog
Who sat on a log
And was about to be studied in school.
He jumped in the water
Saying, "It was a bother
And I'm not that kind of fool."

- End class with a student or two inventing a funny saying about the lesson content that you just taught. For example, after a lesson on communication, one 9th grader observed that "the telegraph was the first text message."
- Use a student's joke before a test or quiz to lower tension.

Small Changes, Big Results

The 10 strategies in this chapter are quite easy to integrate in the classroom, and they can have a significant effect on student motivation. I'm always amazed at what a little drama, humor, reorganization, and freshness can do to change the ho hum to big fun. Continue reading for strategies that, unfortunately, do just the opposite.

3

Twelve Killers of Motivation and Their Remedies

Eliminating practices and procedures that interfere with your students' desire to learn is just as important as implementing and supporting effective motivational practices and procedures. This chapter examines 12 common classroom and school procedures that kill motivation and suggests remedies for each. Some of these killers are implemented by the school district's central office with little or no input from teachers, who then have equally little say about eliminating them from their classrooms. I have identified these cases and offered suggestions for how to live within the boundaries of such policies by stretching them, modifying them, or altering them. Let's start with one of these.

Rigid Curriculum Structure

School districts all over the United States are facing an education crisis due to the number of schools that have been labeled—some correctly, some incorrectly—as failing. I intend no disrespect to the central administrators tasked with finding solutions to this crisis. Frequently, they must contend with too few resources for too many constituencies and with pressure from local, state, and federal agencies. Nonetheless, the distance between them and the classroom is often too great for them to fully understand the effect their choices have on students. Such is the case with highly structured curriculum programs, some of which are so rigid that every teacher must read the exact same words from a prepared script and end the day in the same place as every other teacher using the program.

These programs remove the greatest systemic enhancer of motivation—individualization—and replace it with rigid conformity. The programs go by several names: curriculum mapping, curriculum integration, curriculum alignment, and curriculum scripting. Their goal, however, is the same: to standardize what we teach so that all children have equal opportunity to learn the same content. On the surface, this seems an admirable goal, but it ignores a critical question: should all children learn the same content regardless of their needs, abilities, and circumstances?

Direct Instruction (DI) is an example of this excessive adherence to a "scripted" teaching model that does not allow for individualization. DI is a scripted reading program that in some cases is timed and in all cases builds in the questions for students with no variation on what is acceptable. The program does not allow for student questions. Up until the fall of 2008, the Milwaukee Public Schools, where my colleagues and I were long-term consultants, not only required special education teachers to use a program based on the DI model but also sent DI coordinators into schools to observe teachers and ensure that they were presenting the program precisely as written. The results of this program were bored children and teachers frustrated by the uninteresting content and lack of interaction. Although some students benefited from the highly structured program—teachers told me that one or two students whose learning style happened to align with the principles of DI improved their reading skills with its use—most did not.

The reading program was changed because the Wisconsin Department of Public Instruction (DPI) classified the school district as a District Identified for Improvement. When the DPI conducted an audit of services, it found that the majority of students in special education needed a replacement curriculum. Only students with special needs who participated in statewide testing and whose results were found to be less than proficient were moved out of the DI-modeled program and into the new reading program. Schools were free to continue using Direct Instruction with their regular students and with those special education students whose results met proficiency standards.

When the Milwaukee school system decided to move away from the rigidly structured DI program to a more student-centered approach, one special education administrator observed that "this is still a critical issue, and training is being conducted to get the teachers ready and prepared for the new program. The students and teachers will benefit from this endeavor and, eventually, when results change for the positive, more people will be on board."

In 2008, thanks to pressure from teachers and an administration willing to listen to their concerns, the school system adopted a more flexible reading program. The new program still allows the use of DI for the few students who can benefit from it.

Remedy

When the central administration of an urban district spends many thousands of dollars on a curriculum package, changing the resulting policies is extremely difficult. The remedy in this case is more political than educational: individual or even collective political influence is something teachers typically lack, especially if large sums of money are involved. In urban school districts, curriculum decisions are made at the district level rather than the school level. As the Milwaukee Public Schools example demonstrates, however, it can be done. On a smaller scale, if enough teachers join together and offer a reasonable alternative to curricular decisions that lack flexibility, choice, and creativity, your school or department can introduce a different approach.

When implementing an alternative plan isn't possible, individualize instruction and assessment within the mandated structure as much as you can personally manage. Add to, subtract from, or modify the curriculum to create something tenable. Sometimes we may be restricted in what we teach but have some flexibility in how we teach it. We must always be aware that just because we finish teaching the lesson as scheduled, that doesn't mean that every student finishes learning it as scheduled. This understanding frees us to use more interactive methods to teach otherwise rigid content. I offer suggestions for adopting these methods later in this book.

Obviously, modifying district-approved curriculum involves some risk. I am not asking you to jeopardize your career. Without employing some modifications, however, you may be jeopardizing the motivation of your students.

One Size Fits All (Fair Is Not Equal)

Urban school populations, more than their suburban or rural counterparts, come from diverse backgrounds, speak a variety of languages, and have a host of learning needs. We know that different lessons and academic challenges are necessary to meet students' varying needs and accommodate their differences. Similarly, when dealing with behavior, different consequences are sometimes necessary even when students have violated the same rule. Simply put, if we treat all students in city schools the same, we will fail to motivate and, ultimately, educate them. In the previous chapter, we looked at two very different students—José and Ike—with an identical behavioral problem (failure to do homework). The example of these two students demonstrates that although the outcome we need to address is identical, our solutions must vary due to the different underlying problems leading to each outcome. The following is another example where the one-size-fits-all solution to a behavioral problem does not work.

Sally Blake was a 3rd grade teacher of severely emotionally disturbed and learning-disabled children in Kansas City, Missouri. One of her students, Rachel, had been sexually and physically abused at a very young age and had severe learning difficulties. She was living in a foster care home, one of several she had been placed in over a relatively short period of time. One day, some students teased Rachel. She began crying, lifted up her blouse to expose the scars that still remained from her beatings, and said, "None of you know what it's like to be me; none of y'all were ever beaten like me." The students, shocked by what they saw, formed a circle around her and said, "No one ever insults Rachel again, or they will answer to us. We will protect you, Rachel." Later that day, Rachel sat in Sally's lap and said softly, "You are the only person I can trust, Miss Blake, because I know you will never hurt me."

Shortly after this emotional exchange, Sally caught Rachel stealing items from her pocketbook. Given the connection she believed they had, Sally was livid and considered calling the police. Over the course of several discussions,

Sally and I thoroughly examined the situation, paying particular attention to what Rachel had said. If Sally was the only person Rachel could trust, perhaps she was stealing the items so that she could have a piece of Sally at home to make her feel safe and loved, something she clearly wasn't getting from her foster parents. We decided that Sally would try a unique approach to dealing with Rachel's behavior. With a mix of equal parts hope and anxiety, Sally gave Rachel one of her fancy belts and told Rachel, "Wear this belt whenever you need me and imagine that it is me wrapping my arms around you." Obviously, giving a present to a student who steals is not the norm. But Rachel was not like most students.

A year later, Rachel was institutionalized. Sally went to visit and the staff told her that the belt might have saved Rachel's life. Rachel clutched it during a severe period of depression and kept repeating that Miss Blake loved her. Without the belt, the staff believed, she might not have pulled through. What an incredible affirmation of the power of "fair is not equal."

Remedy

When you apply individually tailored consequences, students may complain that you are being unfair. It is important to explain to your students that *fair* and *equal* do not always mean the same thing. In school, *fair* should be defined as each student getting what he or she needs to succeed and act responsibly. Let your students know that your goal is for each of them to improve his or her learning in your subject every day. Remind them that their improvement should be measured against their own progress, not anyone else's. This clarification is best made before any issue related to individualized instruction or discipline occurs, although it is never too late to discuss it.

It is also helpful to point out to students that the "fair is not equal" concept is already a part of their lives. Invite students to go home and ask their parents, grandparents, or any other adults living in the home to help them make a list of all the examples they can think of that involve treating different people fairly but not equally. Share the results with the class until everyone understands the point you are making. When you are accused of being unfair, explain that you are being "unequal," not unfair.

When deciding on assignments, learning assessments, or consequences for student behavior, use the "one-size-does-*not*-fit-all" concept as often as makes sense. Here are some examples:

• Apply consequences to behavior problems based on what works best with each student. If you know a call home will fall on deaf ears, don't bother. If time out becomes time wasted, use a different method of discipline with that student.

• When giving assignments, allocate a different number of pages to be read or problems to be solved based on each student's ability to meet the learning goal.

• Some students deserve an *A* for answering 90 percent of the questions on a test correctly. Another student, however, might deserve an *A* for answering only 60 percent of the questions correctly, particularly if he typically answers only 20 percent correctly. The jump in correct answers shows individual improvement and should be recognized. Giving this student a *D* will do nothing to promote motivation and may actually kill it.

Boring Teaching Strategies

In 2008, I was invited to observe a second-year 7th grade teacher from San Jose, California. I sat in the back of the room and took out my pen and notepad, ready to take notes. Before long, her monotone voice and uninspired lesson literally put me to sleep. I don't know if she noticed, although I suspect she must have, especially if I snored. Later, we talked about her lesson. "I have to teach this way," she said, "otherwise [the students] will be all over the room and impossible to control." I tried to offer suggestions, but her fear of losing control far outweighed her desire to engage students in her lessons.

Fear of classroom chaos, pressure to improve test scores, the number of inexperienced teachers due to high teacher turnover, and lack of funding for up-to-date textbooks and equipment can all lead to tedious, boring lessons, and boredom is a major killer of motivation. I do not fault teachers for these conditions, but I think more can be done to make classes engaging.

Remedy

The bad news about combating boring lessons is that "boring" is subjective. What one student finds boring might be exciting to another. In addition, some lessons must include drills and repetitive activities that are inherently boring. The good news is that boredom can be kept to a minimum with careful planning and by individualizing the way we teach. The three steps I propose for moving away from boring teaching strategies are all major and long-term. They are all covered in depth in later chapters. But you can—and must—do one thing right now before undertaking these major changes: acknowledge the problem and commit to changing it. These steps are too long and arduous to carry out without a firm commitment:

1. Get control of your class so that interactive lessons do not create chaos. (Chapter 11)

2. Individualize lessons so that all students—regardless of their unique skills, learning styles, and interests—can find energy in what they do. (Chapter 7)

3. Develop lessons that engage, excite, and inspire students to want to learn. (Chapter 7)

Even if you follow these steps most of the time, it is impossible to eliminate all boring lessons. But exhibiting genuine energy and a love of teaching, as well as having trust in your students, can go a long way toward overcoming the effects of the occasional boring lesson.

Ignoring Effort

Aylissa was a new student from Samoa who spoke little English when she arrived in the United States. She studied very hard, did all her work with maximum effort, and stayed after school for extra help. After taking her very first vocabulary test, she proudly told her mother, "When I came to America, I knew none of the words on the test. In three weeks, I learned half of them." Unfortunately, her teacher gave her a 50 percent and Aylissa failed the test.

James, on the other hand, was a bright child with attentive parents. He usually knew all the words well before he was assigned them and frequently got 100 percent or close to it on his vocabulary tests. This time, however, James goofed off and didn't review the vocabulary words before the test. He missed more words than usual but still managed to score a 93 percent and, thus, received an *A*.

The question is: which student really deserved an *A*?

Western culture places a much higher value on achievement than effort. Yet, without effort, a student can never achieve his maximum potential. Students cannot control what they achieve any more than athletes can control whether or not they win. Students can only control how hard they try. Great motivators stress effort, appreciate effort, and encourage effort. When students try their best, achievement takes care of itself. The caveat that I introduced in Chapter 1 still applies, however: effort must be applied correctly if it is to improve learning.

Remedy

I present many remedies for working around the U.S. school system's emphasis on achievement over effort in the chapter on evaluation later in this book. But here's an easy solution to keep in mind for now: compare students against themselves, instead of one another. Using this standard, Aylissa would have gotten the *A* and James a *C*. Imagine being able to say to Aylissa, "I'm glad you tried so hard on this test. You earned an *A*. If you want to get an *A* on the next test, you need to get two more words right. I hope you keep improving." Which approach increases motivation: setting an attainable goal and rewarding Aylissa when she attains it, or failing her, despite the fact that she tried as hard as she could and measurably improved?

Disconnected Lessons

Urban school populations directly reflect the diversity of the cities in which they are situated. Unfortunately, many of the examples teachers have traditionally used to illustrate common subject-area concepts do not resonate with these more culturally and ethnically diverse student bodies. When lessons and assignments fail to resonate with the lives of students, they are of little motivational value. One example of such a disconnect is the teacher who uses coupons to illustrate the concept of percentages in a classroom composed primarily of children who live in poor, ethnic neighborhoods and children who have just come to the United States. If one-third of the class shops at small neighborhood convenience stores that don't give coupons and another third has just arrived from fishing villages in Vietnam where coupons don't exist, then using coupons as an example of the use of percentages is useless. If, on the other hand, the teacher took a tour of the neighborhood stores where her students shopped and took notes on the cost of common items, she could create a lesson to which more of her students would relate.

Of course, it is nearly impossible to make every assignment or lesson relevant to all students' lives, but the more your assignments and lessons connect with students' culture, goals, life experiences, and needs, the greater the chance of engaging them in the process of learning.

Remedy

As I already mentioned, one way to avoid the disconnect between the examples you use in class and your students' lives is to familiarize yourself with your students' neighborhoods. Get an idea of what your students' day-to-day lives are like. This will go a long way toward making you able to create lessons that resonate with them. Another option is to invite a group of parents to help you find quality, relevant examples for your lessons. Perhaps the best way to bridge the disconnect, however, is to ask the students themselves for examples before designing your lessons.

Ineffective Behavioral Interventions

The connection between motivation and behavior is undeniable. Motivated students misbehave infrequently, and unruly students are not typically highly motivated. We do not increase the motivation of those students who don't follow rules with interventions that make them dislike school even more. Urban teachers have legitimate reasons to be highly concerned with behavior and to be more punitive and structured in their responses to misbehavior. Loss of control of the class, messy confrontations, and the gradual erosion of acceptable behavior are all genuine possibilities. Gerri, a frustrated second-year 3rd grade teacher from an urban school, said, "If you give them an inch, they'll take a mile. If you try to correct one student, others jump in and tell you how wrong you are. If I'm not in total control, I have no control at all."

All teachers have the right to expect appropriate behavior in class and school. Further, they have the right to intervene, sometimes strongly, when students violate established rules of conduct. Teachers have choices, however, about what interventions they implement and how they implement them. Some choices lead to improved behavior and increased motivation. Others, unfortunately, get the former by sacrificing the latter.

Remedy

Learn as many interventions as possible so that you have choices of what to do when students break rules. Chapter 11 offers a few of these. For now, when a student misbehaves, try asking yourself the following question before intervening: "If I were on the receiving end of this intervention, delivered in the way I am about to deliver it, would I be more or less likely to be motivated to do my work?" Choose the interventions that at least do not lessen motivation, and try to find those that increase it.

Power Struggles

One of the results of ineffective behavioral interventions is a power struggle. Urban students have a great need to save face. In the neighborhood, backing down is seen as a sign of weakness, leading to the misery of negative labels and, quite possibly, physical harm. This need carries over into school. Students do not want to appear weak to their peers. Many prefer a harsh punishment to backing down from a confrontation with an authority figure. Taking a punishment shows bravery in the face of authority, an attribute highly regarded in many urban neighborhoods.

Teachers, also, may prefer negative results to backing down and being seen as weak by their students. When a power struggle begins, three possible outcomes exist: (1) The teacher says something like "Right now we are headed for a power struggle. Both of us will be unhappy if we continue, and I don't want that.

Let's take a break and find another way to resolve this so that no one loses." (2) The student says something like "Right now we are headed for a power struggle. Both of us will be unhappy if we continue, and I don't want that. Let's take a break and find another way to resolve this so that no one loses." (3) The struggle continues forever. Realistically, it is unlikely that (2) will occur, which leaves two choices: either the teacher stops the conflict or the conflict doesn't stop. Do you think a teacher sets a good example as an adult role model by engaging in arguments with students in front of the class? If the teacher wins and the student gives in and does what the teacher wanted in the first place, how motivated to learn do you think that student will be?

Of course, defusing power struggles is easier said than done. I learned this lesson the hard way as a consultant in a largely Hispanic middle school in San Jose, California. The school neighborhood was gang- and drug-infested, and many of the students' parents were either in prison or had served prison time. While I was walking through the school with the assistant principal, we came across a teacher involved in an argument with Hector, an angry 7th grader. Culminating what had obviously been a heated exchange, Hector said to the teacher, "You're a damn liar! Liar, liar, liar!" The teacher threatened to hold Hector back for a year if he did not apologize, to which Hector responded by calling her a liar once more.

I asked if I could talk with Hector privately for a moment. The teacher replied, "Somebody better talk to him," and walked away in a huff. Hector and I went into an empty room to chat. "This is my big chance," I thought. "Now I can show the school how to skillfully handle a severe power struggle." After some small talk about baseball, I turned the conversation to the exchange I had just witnessed:

Me: Why are you so angry with that teacher, Hector?

Hector: Because she insulted me.

Me: Is it wrong to insult people?

Hector: Yes.

Me. Is it always wrong to insult people?

Hector: Yes.

Me: But you insulted your teacher when you called her a liar. Does that mean you are wrong?

Hector: That's different.

Eventually, Hector acknowledged that he could have handled the situation better and agreed to learn different words to express his unhappiness. We spent about 15 minutes practicing how he would apologize to his teacher without negating his own feelings about the situation: "I'm sorry I called you a liar, but I still think you're wrong."

Hector said he was ready, so we went and knocked on the teacher's door. When she came out into the hallway, I said that Hector had something to tell her.

Hector looked at me and smiled, then looked at her and said, "You're a damn fucking liar."

I was shocked. "That's not what we practiced," I stammered.

Hector replied, "Who the hell are you? She's a liar and I'm not changing my mind."

So much for demonstrating my great skills! I learned once again that if a child does not want to change, we cannot make him. The best way to resolve power struggles is to avoid getting into them. But they ignite fast and escalate faster. By the time we realize the trouble we are in, it is often too late.

Remedy

Try these four steps when you sense a power struggle brewing:

1. Acknowledge the student's feelings.
2. Agree with the part that the student is right about.
3. State that you care too much about that student and about resolving the situation to fight.
4. Set up a time to talk later.

The following sample dialogue uses the four steps for defusing a potential power struggle:

Teacher: Eli, people are not for hitting. We'll talk about this after school.

Eli: She called me a bad name, so I'm gonna hit her. And I ain't stayin' after no school.

Acknowledge the student's feelings.

Teacher: You must be very upset to talk to me that way.

Agree with the part that the student is right about.
Teacher: And I agree that you have every right to defend yourself when other students call you names. But hitting is not an acceptable solution.

State that you care too much to fight.
Teacher: I do not want to get in an argument with you about this because I care too much about you.

Set up a time to talk later.
Teacher: When we meet after school, we can think of some great ways of handling a situation like this without breaking the rules or hurting other people.

Broken Connections Between School and Home

We have already discussed the disastrous effects that a lack of support in the home can have on students. Regardless of whether I'm speaking in an urban or a suburban setting, I always get a round of enthusiastic applause when I say to an audience of teachers that students don't present the greatest behavior challenge; parents do. Suburban "problem parents" are demanding, accusatory, and prone to blaming everyone else—especially the teacher—for their child's poor choices. As Al Mendler, my frequent coauthor, points out, "Sadly, some well-educated parents may actually frown upon teachers whom they view as relatively poorly paid and therefore unworthy of respect in our highly materialistic society" (2006). The situation is far more complicated in urban settings. The high numbers of non-English-speaking parents or parents who speak English as a second language make communication between teachers and family a challenge. In addition, the high numbers of homes in which both parents work or single-parent homes in which the parent works odd or long hours make parent-teacher conferences difficult to schedule. Many of the parents who create problems on a personal level—unrelated to language barriers and scheduling issues—had negative experiences when they were in school, and these affect their current feelings about their children's situation. And then there is the ever-present specter of racism, whether real or imagined, overt or subtle.

When the messages students receive at home and at school are in agreement with regard to goals, strategies, and behavior, students usually perform at a high level, both academically and behaviorally. When problems occur, they are solved with mutual respect and understanding among school officials, parents, and students. When a disconnect between home and school exists, on the other hand, and students receive mixed messages between the two, their desire and need to perform their best is reduced, sometimes dramatically so. Some parents actively undermine both the goals and strategies of school. Every urban teacher has heard from at least one student who says, "My dad says it's OK to hit. I have a right to hit." In addition, it's hard to imagine students feeling motivated when their parents don't ask about school (or when they make disparaging remarks about it), don't check to see if their homework has been completed, don't read with or to them, and don't seem to care about the results of projects or tests. To complicate matters further, children almost universally respond to and internalize the messages, both verbal and nonverbal, offered by their parents, even when those messages are negative and unsupportive. Children's desire to please their parents, even in abusive situations, frequently trumps their motivation to succeed in school. This puts teachers and administrators in a difficult position, but the responsibility to provide a positive, supportive environment for children, regardless of the state of their home lives, is paramount.

Remedy

Of course, not all problem parents lack an interest in—or seek to undermine— their children's education; some parents are simply uncomfortable communicating with school officials, whether because of language barriers, social anxiety, or feelings of inadequacy in educational settings. Set up a voicemail system so that parents who are embarrassed in any way or uncomfortable coming to school or talking on the phone can communicate with you. This has proven effective in many urban schools I have visited.

Send special invitations to Parent Night to encourage attendance among parents who don't normally come to school functions. With parents who seem to have a negative opinion of school, acknowledge that although they may have had a difficult school experience growing up, you hope to keep that from being their children's experience. Be sure to have interpreters available if needed.

Be careful not to make assumptions about parents. I can speak from personal experience on this point. I went on a road trip when my son was in high school and asked him to do the dishes while I was gone. Unfortunately, his idea of doing dishes was to add more to the pile already in the sink. I arrived home from my trip at 2 a.m., threw my dirty clothes all over the living room while looking through my suitcase for my medications, and went to sleep. Later that morning, my son's teacher dropped by our house to talk. Given the mess in the kitchen and the clothes all over the floor, I was too embarrassed to meet with her. I was also half asleep and undoubtedly came off as rude as I told her as much. I'm sure she had some negative things to say about me in the faculty room. My experience demonstrates that there may be situations in which appearances do not match reality.

Setting up a positive relationship with parents before any problems occur can go a long way toward gaining their support when a problem does present itself. Consider leaving parents a message at the beginning of the school year that establishes your desire to support their child. Here's an example: "Hello, Mr. Prague, I'm Lauren's teacher. I want Lauren to have a great year, and I intend to do everything I can to help her succeed. Please feel free to contact me or visit me at school if you need to talk, and I will contact you to let you know how things are going for Lauren."

Make a list of students whose parents might need to be called about a problem at some point. Prioritize your list and call a reasonable number of parents each week (three to eight) based on your schedule.

Setting Expectations Too Low or Too High

Expectations can have a powerful effect on motivation and effort. Ironically, for many urban students, expectations are set both too high *and* too low. When our expectations are too low, students believe that they are unable to perform at a higher level. The expectation creates an artificial ceiling. When expectations are too high, however, students cannot meet them and feel like failures, both to themselves and to others.

We present our lowered expectations in numerous ways, from the *structural* (e.g., placing students in predetermined homogeneous ability groups), to the *formal* (e.g., officially recognizing honor roll students at a school assembly), to the *informal* (e.g., only calling on the "good" students or telling a student to "just do the best you can").

Having lower expectations for students' performance often results in giving them less challenging work, and being able to complete easier work does not lead to a sense of pride or achievement. When was the last time you felt a sense of pride over completing an easy task? Motivation increases when teachers raise their academic expectations for students. On the other hand, when expectations are too high and, thus, beyond the reach of students, motivation also suffers. Students should never be penalized, either formally or informally, for not being successful at work they are unable to do. Care must be taken to differentiate between what students truly cannot do and what they can do but incorrectly believe they cannot. Encouraging students to try to do difficult work is helpful to motivation; punishing them for not being able to do it with low grades, verbal accusations, or negativity is not.

Remedy

Like curricula, expectations and their formal cousin, standards, work best when they are individualized. All students need encouragement to achieve at a high level without fear of being labeled a failure if expectations are set too high. Let students find their own level of challenge whenever possible. (The appendixes at the back of this book offer "challenge sheets" that allow students to do this.)

Given that our expectations for students can affect their levels of effort and motivation, it is perhaps unsurprising that the ways in which we interact with students can profoundly affect their performance level. The Teacher Expectations and Student Achievement (TESA) program, a research-based inservice training program for K–12 teachers, identified a number of teacher behaviors and techniques that can improve how well students perform (Kerman, Kimball, & Martin, 1980). These include

- Equitable distribution of attention for all students.
- Affirmation and correction of student performance.
- Proximity of the teacher to students during learning activities.
- Individual help for those who need it.
- Positive reinforcement and praise of student performance.

- Courtesy and consistency.
- Latency, or allowing time for learning or mastery to occur.
- Demonstration of a personal interest in the true welfare of students.
- An effort to mine students' lives outside school for information that can make lessons more relevant.
- Careful listening and an attempt to truly understand what students are trying to say.
- Appropriate and professional physical contact with students.
- Higher-level questioning and higher expectations of student performance.
- Acceptance of students' feelings and nonjudgmental empathy for students.
- Ability to effectively stop inappropriate student behavior.

Inappropriate Standards

Standards are, essentially, a formalized version of expectations; they are expectations codified into an evaluation tool to measure student achievement and judge if it is sufficient. While expectations affect learning, standards affect lives in a more direct, tangible manner. They can determine grade placement, college acceptance, graduation rates, and career choices. Unfortunately, standards have become a measure of accountability for teachers and schools as well. Urban schools, especially those in large cities with intractable bureaucracies, continually struggle with the sizable gap between the people who set and enforce standards and the teachers who must meet them.

I am a strong believer in standards. They are an essential part of ensuring that students have something to work toward, and in that sense, they are a motivator. I do not believe that all answers are right, that students can or should be the only judges of their own success, or that evaluation can only be implied. My argument is not with standards but with how they are applied. Because the power standards have to profoundly affect the lives and future of students, the seriousness of misuse or misapplication of standards cannot be underestimated. For no one is this truer than for inner-city students. Urban schools have such a wide variety of students with diverse needs, conditions, and family lives that it is preposterous to employ the same standards for all students.

I strongly believe that school is not just for good students; school is for all students, and standards must be individualized accordingly. What good is a standard that causes a student who does his best to fail? If we assume that our primary goal is for all students to learn as much as they can, then standards must be based on what each student can learn. When the school requires students to achieve beyond their ability, the problem is with the school, not the child. Failing students because they do not meet an artificial standard only stops further learning. It does not make them try harder. If we can develop IEPs for some students, then we can create individualized standards for all. Individualizing standards does not make them inoperable, nor does it "water them down." Individualizing standards makes them functional. It does not make sense to apply the same standards to a student in advanced classes who plans to attend a four-year college and to a student in basic classes who wants to become a mechanic. Both paths are equally valid, but they do not require the application of the same educational standards. How can we tell students that they can pass our courses if they try, only to have them fail an arbitrary school, state, or national standard that has nothing to do with their future?

Some states do have different standards for students with disabilities but then negate this individualization by clumping all disabilities into one category. Hearing-impaired students, emotionally dysfunctional students, and students on the autism spectrum are all required to meet the same standards. We can easily see that this expectation is unreasonable. Why should it be different for students who are not disabled?

Remedy

Unfortunately, teachers and even school administrators have little control over city, state, or federal standards. What we *can* do is attempt to motivate students to do their best as much of the time as possible. We can encourage them and build hope, and we can challenge them to continue trying to achieve at the highest level of which they are capable. Keep in mind that learning something is better than learning nothing. It is your responsibility to do what is best for students, not for those who set inappropriate standards.

A teacher I met in Chicago said it best: "I used to worry about test scores all the time. I pushed upstream to finish the curriculum and taught for the test much of the time. I began to yell a lot and stopped loving my work. My scores were never high enough to please anyone. I finally shifted my focus back to what I loved. I stopped worrying about tests, scores, and the curriculum. I just taught what I loved with love and let the chips fall where they may. Wonder of wonders, my scores sharply improved, my life improved, and I've been teaching this way ever since."

Labeling

Labels can be useful shorthand to help professionals communicate quickly and efficiently. If everything had to be spelled out in detail, exchanging information would be a tedious operation indeed. But labels also determine expectations, pass on potentially inaccurate judgments, and box students in mentally—all of which are detrimental to motivation. Labeling a student as lazy, underachieving, a troublemaker, a dummy, an attention seeker, or a gangster perpetuates negativity and can create a self-fulfilling prophecy. If a student is consistently labeled a low achiever, she may begin to self-identify as such and will potentially stop trying to be something more. Except in situations where a student must be labeled in an official capacity to get special assistance or access to extra services, avoid using labels and try to ignore them when you hear other teachers use them. Even in these special cases, the "official" label should not affect your relationship with the student.

Remedy

Try doing a substitution when you are tempted to use a label or when you hear another teacher use one. When you want to say that a student is arrogant, for example, try "She defends herself" instead. Rather than calling a student a gangster, consider saying "That student has troublesome friends." If you find yourself starting to describe a student as lazy, switch to "I've yet to find the key to involving her."

Make a list of commonly used labels—both labels that you use and ones you've heard used—and find reasonable substitutes for them.

Inflexible Policies

Policies help decision makers figure out the best, fairest way to handle individual situations. They are meant to be guidelines, not laws. In urban schools, policies primarily focus on safety issues, including lockdown procedures, ways to deal with gang and drug behavior, and detection of weapons. Of course, as in other schools, urban school policies also address issues such as curriculum, evaluation, and interaction with parents.

The best school policies help everyone involved—teachers, administrators, parents, and students. When conflicts arise among these groups, good policies make the situation tenable to as many of the involved parties as possible. They are flexible, allowing for the reality that similar situations may call for very different solutions. Flexibility is crucial. Inflexible policies may address a good number of situations, but they do not allow for out-of-the-ordinary circumstances. They do not allow for individualization. These policies wind up sacrificing the best interests of all parties involved. An example of such a nonsensical policy is "zero tolerance." The following example provides insight into why zero tolerance and other inflexible policies can do more harm than good.

Freddy, an 11th grader, and his younger brother were living with their alcoholic, abusive father. Freddy drove his brother to school every morning because his father was usually unable or unwilling to do so. One morning, the boys' father came home drunk, brandishing a handgun. He pointed the gun at Freddy and said, "I'm going to kill you and your brother. I hate both of you." Then he passed out on the floor. Freddy quickly put the gun in his backpack and, extremely shaken, drove his brother to school. When he arrived at his own school, he ran to the principal's office to give her the gun and ask for advice. A teacher stopped him for running and discovered the gun. The zero tolerance policy required the school to expel him, a decision that was clearly inappropriate in this situation. After a drawn-out battle, the principal was able to reverse the decision, but Freddy's initial experience makes clear that any policy that fails to include options to match individual circumstances can wind up doing a great deal of harm. Imagine if Freddy had not had the principal fighting for him? Likewise, any policy that begins with the concept of "mandatory" is usually ineffective. As with standards, lesson plans, and our expectations for student performance, the concept of "fair is not equal" also applies to policymaking.

Remedy

A policy's effectiveness is more dependent on how it is implemented and interpreted than on its content. Avoid thinking "That's the policy. There is nothing I can do." Replace that thought with "This is the policy. Let's see how we can use it to help resolve this situation in the best possible way."

Parsing the Problems

An examination of the 12 problems discussed in this chapter reveals multiple connections among them. For example, policymaking and the idea of one-size-fits-all are integrally connected. Labeling leads to expectations, and vice versa. Degree of student effort should be considered when designing and applying standards. And so on. For the sake of simplicity of organization, I have dealt with each one separately, but in real life, they frequently overlap. Despite the many ways in which these topics could have been arranged, I hope the way I have categorized and discussed them makes sense to you. More to the point, I hope you find the remedies I offer indispensable in dealing with these problems.

4

Punishments, Threats, and Rewards

Teachers frequently come to me with a familiar lament: "It is so hard to get students to do their work. If I can get them to do their work and learn from it, does it really matter if they are motivated?" This seemingly simple query gets at the very definition of learning and brings up the larger question of cost versus benefit. If a technique gets a student to learn, but at a very rudimentary level, is that good enough? What if the student could learn more with another technique? Was the learning worth the cost? If a student learns but also learns to despise the subject in the process, was the learning worth the cost? If a student learns but only through the use of techniques that foster habits that will hinder learning in the future (e.g., providing external rewards—toys, gold stars, special privileges—rather than encouraging internal motivation), was the learning worth the cost?

Choosing any educational strategy requires two essential considerations: (1) its benefit and (2) its cost. I often hear things like "It works" or "Research proves positive results." Be wary of those who cite research to prove their point on this issue. For example, a doctor could amputate my leg to stop a pain in my knee. It will work—and research will verify that it worked—but at what cost? Often, the benefit is obvious, but the cost is hidden.

Let's examine one such strategy. I used to say things like "Class, I like the way Armando is sitting" or "Class, I like the way Ruthie has her book open and is ready to learn." I learned this strategy when I was a college student training to be a teacher, and I thought it was fabulous. I used it as a student teacher, and my master teacher loved it, too. When I was up for tenure, my principal put it in the "plus" column on my evaluation. I taught it to my students when I was a college instructor training new teachers. Then I discovered its hidden cost.

Teachers use strategies like these every day. As they were with me, they may even be among your favorite strategies for eliciting desired behavior from your students. The benefit is obvious. Other students sit down or get out their books in preparation for the lesson. But there are costs as well. First, when we employ this strategy, we are being manipulative. Pointing out that we like the way Armando is sitting is really just a roundabout way of saying, "Class, sit down." Why can't we simply tell students what we want directly and honestly? If we don't want students to manipulate us, it doesn't make sense to teach them to manipulate by example. Second, we are teaching students that in order to be liked, they must do what others want them to do. I prefer to teach students that they need to make good choices, regardless of whether those choices are popular. Third, it alienates the students who never get singled out for praise— hardly an effective motivator.

Threats, punishments, and rewards must be similarly examined. When we hear that a strategy employing any of these works, we must ask, "Maybe it does, but at what cost?"

Clearly, as evidenced by my desire to write this book, I believe that it is far better to try to motivate students than to simply get them to do work. However, I also firmly believe that *learning something is better than learning nothing.* If the only way to create learning is to use techniques that do not inspire motivation, then these techniques are acceptable. But they should be viewed as a last resort rather than as everyday classroom strategies. It is always preferable to find what motivates a student and use that to generate learning. Teachers frequently fall back on threats and punishments (or a combination of the two) to get students to do their work. Let's take a look at what is wrong with these strategies, examine how they are particularly troublesome in urban settings, and discuss what can take their place.

Threats and Punishments

Urban students face threats every day, most of them far more serious than any a teacher could make. Threats from gang members, junkies, and drug dealers are part of the neighborhood landscape. Many are threatened by the police or by their parents, the very people who are supposed to protect them. So it makes little sense to threaten them at school.

The threats available to teachers cannot compete with these real-life threats. The least motivated students don't care about threats. Lucas was a sophomore in high school who returned to regular school after a year in a lockdown facility in Indianapolis, Indiana. He learned to like the lockdown because he was fed regularly, was safer there than he had been at home, and had a predictable, structured life. What threat could a teacher possibly use to get Lucas to do his work? Detention? A call home? A failing grade? Sending him back to a place he liked? Further, shouldn't we try to reduce threats for our most beleaguered students?

Even with cases less extreme than Lucas's, threats do not work. Over time, they satiate. The first time Marti, a 3rd grader from Oakland, California, got a detention, she begged for mercy: "Please, Mrs. Deleen. If you don't give me a detention, I promise to never do it again. Please!" By the time she got her fourth detention, however, Marti's response was, "Cool, I like detentions. Why not give me a hundred? I don't care. All my friends will be there, too."

When threats have no effect, we tend to increase the punishment rather than find a different method. If one detention does not work, maybe five will. If a two-day suspension is insufficient, then give a five-day suspension. What if medicine worked this way? What if, when we discovered that a treatment was ineffective (or even harmful), we doubled it, instead of finding a treatment that actually worked?

We've all heard the saying "Fear is a great motivator." If we define motivation simply as "that which gets us to do things," then this statement is certainly true. Fear of punishment or consequences can get us to do a great many things, including schoolwork. And threats, if taken seriously, can lead to fear. But we are not defining motivation in this way here. Far from cultivating motivation, threats can, in fact, kill it:

- Threats lead to finishing, not learning.
- Threats lead to an "I have to" mentality, not an "I want to" mentality.
- Threats satiate, requiring the use of stronger and stronger threats over time.

At what point do we run out of effective inducements to fear? And how much fear does the threat of low grades elicit in students who never receive anything higher than a *D* or an *F*?

Low grades are a consequence of not being motivated enough to perform adequately. Many educators believe that it is OK to give out assignments and step back, abdicating further responsibility for the outcome. More than once, I've heard, "If students fail because they don't do anything, then it is their fault. Let them fail. It will teach them a good lesson." The truth is, it teaches them a "bad" lesson; it fails to foster motivation and, in fact, can kill what little existing motivation a student might have. Our responsibility as teachers goes beyond simply presenting information. If our students don't learn, then we haven't done our job. Presenting information is just one part of the equation.

Teachers frequently use threats unknowingly. These "hidden" threats are disguised as choices. A choice is genuine if (1) we have no preference as to what students choose and (2) none of the choices are punishments. The inclusion of punishment turns the choice into a threat. Let's look at some examples:

- You can do your homework or get a zero; the choice is yours.
- If you don't put that cell phone away, I'll call your mother; the choice is yours.
- You can either stop talking or go to the principal's office.

These all sound like choices because they offer two alternatives, but they are really threats. In each example, we know which choice we want the student to make; the other choice is a punishment. If the student does what we want, it's because he has to, not because he wants to. And what if the student does not do what we want? Obviously, the preferable outcome is for the student to learn, but by making a threat, we back ourselves into a corner if the student fails to comply. We then feel that we must follow through on the threat, and once that happens, any possible opportunity for learning disappears. Although threats are sometimes necessary, especially when someone's safety is at risk (e.g., "Stop or I'll call the police!"), they are rarely appropriate in an academic setting, and they do not motivate.

Adding to the confusion, we frequently use the words *consequence* and *punishment* interchangeably even though they are very different. Consequences come as a result of choices, whereas punishments are the end result of threats. A punishment is what is done to us, either to make us pay for something we've done or to deter us from doing it again. If I'm late getting to the airport, a punishment would be to announce to the entire waiting area that I am incapable of arriving at the airport in a timely manner, thereby embarrassing me in front of a room of strangers. This is not a natural outcome. It is something the airline or ticketing agent chose to do to me in order to deter me from being late again. A consequence, on the other hand, is the natural result of the choices we make. No one imposes it on us. In a sense, we do it to ourselves. If I am late to the airport, I miss my flight. No one chooses to make me miss my flight. It happens as a natural result of failing to get to the airport on time. Take a look at the following examples of punishments and consequences. Can you distinguish one from the other?

1. A student is sent to the office for fighting.

2. A student does not learn a math concept because he was late for class.

3. A student is not accepted into a school club because he habitually insults people.

4. A student must publically apologize to the class for creating a disruption during the lesson.

Answers: 1. punishment, 2. consequence, 3. consequence, 4. punishment

Consequences may feel like punishments in that they often don't feel good and can make a student miserable, but as long as the misery is self-created, it is still a consequence.

Replacing Threats with Choices

Using threats will be a difficult habit to break, especially when you don't necessarily realize that you are making a threat instead of offering a choice. You can distinguish between the two by remembering the two points discussed above. Ask yourself if you have a preference as to which option is chosen and then examine whether any of the options are punishments. Here are some examples of choices to guide you:

- If you don't do your work now, you can do it during lunchtime when it's quiet in the classroom, during recess, or during our free reading period. Which do you chose?
- You haven't done your homework for a week now. I know you have very little time at home to get it done, so for this week, you can complete numbers 1, 4, and 7; numbers 2, 5, and 8; or numbers 3, 6, and 9. Which set will you do?
- Because your disruptive behavior took up so much class time today, you owe us time back. For the next three days, I want you to help a student who is having trouble understanding this lesson. Here are the names of the students who can benefit from your help. Whom do you choose?
- I know you don't like to read aloud in class, so let's think about ways you can demonstrate your reading ability. You can read to me privately, pick another student you trust and read to him, or record yourself reading. Which would you prefer?

It is not always easy to find choices that work for a particular student. But think of it this way. If you use a threat, you may get the same answer: "Who cares? I'm still not going to do what you want." So why not leave your options—and your students' options—open and offer a choice instead?

Likewise, when you give a student a warning, stress consequences, not punishments. It is not a threat to warn a student about a negative consequence, provided the outcome really is a consequence. Telling a student, "If you don't wear a coat, you may be cold," for example, is different from saying, "If you don't wear a coat and get cold, I won't let you come back for one. That might teach you to listen to me!" Telling a student, "If you don't do your homework, you might not understand tomorrow's lesson" or "If you don't listen, you won't understand what is going on in class" apprises the student of the consequences of her behavior and offers her a choice of how to proceed.

Bribes

I hear a variety of arguments for rewarding urban students when they do well academically or behaviorally. One argument goes thus: "So many urban kids are deprived of positive reinforcement. They never get rewarded for doing well. Often, they never even get noticed. They need and deserve rewards." I've also had teachers argue that rewards get students to learn needed skills. And they're not punishments, so what's the problem? Although I agree that urban students' lives frequently lack positive reinforcement and that offering rewards can, indeed, compel students to do their work, rewards do not necessarily result in learning. If a reward is offered to solicit specific behavior, even desirable behavior, it is little more than a bribe, and bribes are not effective motivators. Looked at another way, bribes are simply threats in disguise. If I say to you, "If you do everything in this book, I'll give you a sticker to put on the cover," what I'm really saying is, "If you don't do what I say, I will deny you a sticker." The truth is that threats and bribes are two sides of the same coin: control.

Recently, rewarding students for academic achievement reached new heights (or lows) with the trend of actually paying students for good grades. Certainly, Chicago's Green for Grade$ program and New York City's Spark program, among others, may lead some students' grades to improve, but at what cost? Bribing students pushes them to achieve at the cost of real understanding, encourages them to be "finishers" (and possibly even cheaters) rather than learners, and sends the dangerous message that desirable behavior is a commodity to be bought and sold. Further, there will always be students who are unable to meet the requirements set for rewards, even when they try their best. Hence, they find themselves in yet another situation in which they are overlooked. How is this in any way motivating?

We can divide the concept of "rewards" into two categories: appreciation and bribes. What students need is the former; what they do not need are the latter. All students need positive recognition. They need to know that we notice their achievements and, especially, their effort. When appreciation does not have to be earned, it is a wonderful motivator. Appreciation should not be expected in advance, nor should it be held back until students do what we want. When we express appreciation for something a student has done, we are expressing genuine feelings, with no underlying manipulation. Compare this with bribery.

There are times when bribing a student is the right thing to do. Some students, due to severe learning or social disabilities, will never lead independent lives. They will never have a romantic relationship, hold a job, or live alone without assistance. For these children, the negatives of bribery are insignificant compared with the benefit of basic skill development. Any method that helps them learn to function is for the good. For nearly all other students, however, bribery has too many negative side effects to be a first choice as a classroom strategy. Let's take a look at some of these negative side effects.

Satiation. Over time, students demand more and more rewards to perform the same activities. They never say, "That's way too much. Please give me less." It's always, "Is that all? I want more." Eventually, students start to expect rewards, and all the stickers, food, ribbons, and parties lose their power to elicit desired behavior. You can't start students down the path of learning by providing external rewards and later switch to internal rewards. Starting with external rewards only leads to the desire for more external rewards.

Addiction. Many students become addicted to rewards and will not work without them. When I taught 7th grade English, I frequently gave stickers to my students. One day I ran out and informed the class that there would be no stickers for a few days. A near riot ensued. "Where's my sticker?" "I want a sticker!" "I won't do anything without a sticker!!!" A parent even called me that night to complain that her son was upset because I hadn't given him his sticker! I realized my students had become addicted to stickers. The next day, I investigated how much money is spent on stickers in U.S. schools. It was in the millions! I thought how much better spent that money could be on improving the quality of education. I decided never to use stickers again.

Granted, calling students' dependence on rewards "addiction" is a bit of an exaggeration, but there is an addictive quality to rewards. If you bribe students with rewards—whether stickers or ribbons or special privileges—see what happens when you tell your students you're no longer going to use them. Odds are they will be very upset.

Finishing. Learning from a lesson and simply finishing it are very different things. Did you take and pass a foreign language course in high school or college? Can you speak that language now? Have you ever taken a required course and passed it but learned little or nothing in the process? This phenomenon is called "finishing." Bribes tend to produce finishers rather than learners. Students are more interested in finishing their work and getting the proffered reward than actually learning what the lesson is designed to teach.

Manipulation. We do not like it when students try to manipulate us. Yet we frequently employ manipulation as a classroom strategy, thereby teaching them by example to be master manipulators. Sometimes it is hard to tell the difference between manipulating and appreciating because the action is the same. Ms. Oates told her 9th grade student Helen, "I am so proud of the way you sat down when the bell rang and got ready to work." Was this a manipulation or an appreciation? The answer lies in the intent. Was Ms. Oates simply happy about what Helen did, or was she trying to get her to do it again? Admittedly, the motive behind such a statement is frequently a combination of both genuine appreciation and manipulation, but one generally outweighs the other.

Giving your partner flowers illustrates the appreciation versus manipulation concept. If the flowers are meant to show your love for the recipient, the gesture is appreciation. If they are meant to convince the recipient to do you a favor, it is manipulation. Many urban students have been manipulated throughout their academic careers and are understandably attuned to it. Not surprisingly, their reaction to it tends to be negative.

Winners sometimes lose. Maria was a personable 8th grader who studied hard and gave thoughtful answers in class. Her teacher continually singled her out, saying, "Why can't more of you be like Maria? She always does her work and tries hard." Eventually, Maria's classmates began to tease her about being the teacher's pet. She was occasionally even shunned. She began doing minor, annoying things in class and stopped handing in homework in order to get the teacher to stop using her as an example and, thus, to stop the persecution from her fellow students. Maria's reaction is not uncommon. Many students are uncomfortable about being singled out for doing well, particularly if it leads to social ostracization.

Bribes reduce choices. When we offer an incentive for a student to do something, we are deciding for that student what we want him to do. This is not inherently negative; often, we need to make decisions for students, especially those involving safety. But when we make decisions for others, we take away their ability to make a choice and we lose an opportunity to teach decision-making skills. One way to identify great teachers is by how well they balance telling students what to do with letting them make their own choices. I lean heavily toward letting students make their own choices rather than telling them what to do, but the circumstances must be the final determiner.

An Experiment

If you want proof that internal rewards cannot easily replace external rewards, try the following experiment. Ask your students to write a short paragraph about something you know is of interest to them. Make it a voluntary assignment with neither negative nor positive consequences. Tell them, "This is only to help you." See how many students complete the assignment, and examine the quality of their work. About two weeks later, do the same thing, but this time tell the class that anyone who completes the assignment will get an *A*, regardless of the quality of their work. See if the number of students who complete the assignment increases, but the quality suffers. About a week later, offer the same assignment but go back to the original structure—no consequences, no grades. See if the number of students who complete the assignment is the same as it was when you offered an *A*, regardless of quality. You will likely find that students respond, "It's not worth it. What will I get in return?" The need for an external reward, in this case an *A*, has trumped the internal reward, the desire to improve or learn. Once a student has received a bribe, he or she almost always wants more, not less.

Break the Reward Addiction

There are two ways to break any addiction: cold turkey or step down. With my 7th grade class and their sticker addiction, I opted for cold turkey. I told my class that only little kids used stickers. Smart 7th graders didn't need them. They were too mature and intelligent. "But," I added, "maybe there are some immature, less intelligent kids in this class who still need stickers. If any of you are like that, raise your hand and I'll be sure to give you stickers whenever you want." No one raised a hand and that was the end, thankfully, of sticker addiction in my class. This incident obviously took place before I realized the long-term effects of using manipulation to elicit desired behavior. Still, correlating stickers with immaturity is not a giant leap; it's a truth that students can learn.

The step down method is the gradual removal of the reward until it disappears. Use rewards less each week until the students no longer need them. Breaking addiction is not easy. Most of you have either broken an addiction—smoking, drinking, overeating, drugs—or know someone who has. There is a significant period of difficulty and discomfort and desire for the addictive agent. The same will happen in your class if you switch from rewards to appreciation. Students may do less work, exhibit stubbornness, and even act out for a time. Some teachers see this as a sign that making the switch is not working. Not so. It is a natural effect of withdrawal, and if you stay with it, your students will get over it, just as with any addiction.

Increase Appreciation

Make a point of noticing good behavior, appreciating it, encouraging it, and sharing how you feel about it. Do this as often as is appropriate. Your students, especially those deprived of appreciation, need it. It is not always easy to tell the difference between praise, which can be used as a bribe, and enthusiastic encouragement. One question can help distinguish between the two: Is what you are saying or doing a genuine expression of how you feel, or are you just trying to get the student to repeat her behavior? This is not necessarily an easy question to answer. Most of the time, we are motivated both by genuine feeling and by a desire to elicit the same behavior again. It is not a matter of either/or but rather one of degree. Practice asking yourself this question when you talk with students and you will get better at answering it.

Do No Harm

When deciding whether to use threats, punishments, and rewards, think like a physician: first, do no harm. Think through the result of using these techniques and ask yourself if they might make the situation worse. If so, it is best to find another strategy. Sticking with the medical analogy, minimally invasive techniques are always preferable to those that are more invasive. Threats, punishments, and rewards are highly invasive due to the number of negative outcomes that can result from using them. They should only be considered if there are no other options.

5

Creating Hope in Students

Hope—the belief that things can get better—is the foundation upon which motivation is built. In urban schools, hope requires two beliefs: (1) that life can be better for students and better than it was for their parents, and (2) that success in school can help pave the way to that better life. The opposite of hope is cynicism. The first step toward creating hope is to remove institutional cynicism from schools. Once institutional cynicism takes hold of a school, it breeds decisions and policies based on fear rather than love. And, unfortunately, it is all too common in urban schools.

During a 2008 visit to an inner-city school that will remain unnamed, I was introduced to the vice principal. The first words out of her mouth were that most of her students were crazy and in need of psychological treatment. At first I thought she was using "crazy" colloquially and meant it as an expression of endearment, but I soon realized that she actually meant insane. She was in charge of handling behavior problems in the school, and the principal later told me that, not surprisingly, the students behaved better when the vice principal was not in the building. Such negativity is corrosive. It bleeds over onto other administrators and teachers and telegraphs itself to students, who implicitly understand that they have, in effect, been dismissed.

Teachers and administrators who have given up create institutional cynicism. They are not bad people; they just do not belong in schools. When I taught student teachers at San Francisco State University, I told my students that they would fail if they spent more than one day talking to a cynical teacher. Although I was obviously employing hyperbole, I nonetheless got my point across.

I recall making a major presentation in Chicago to several hundred teachers. At the beginning of my talk, a man in the back of the large meeting room asked me, "What is professionalism?" I started to give a long-winded, jargon-filled answer, when he interrupted me. "No, no," he said, "I mean is it professional to make me come to this useless, stupid presentation?" Many in the audience nodded their heads in agreement. Recognizing the cynicism in his voice and seeing the audience reaction, I answered, "No, it is not professional to force any of you to be here, but because great teachers know that today you might learn something to help children learn, I'm glad you're here." He left shortly thereafter.

We generate hope by being hopeful ourselves. Joan Kristall, a social worker from Baltimore who treats severe trauma victims, tells them, "If you cannot feel hope, then let me hold it in my heart for you until you are ready to claim it for yourself." We can offer the same custodianship for those children who have yet to feel hopeful about school. Admittedly, this is sometimes hard to do in inner-city schools. It is what separates the good teachers from the great ones. All teachers can fight institutional cynicism in their school by confronting it, working to reduce it, and acknowledging their own frustrations, which, if allowed to fester, can lead to cynicism. Here are three strategies for accomplishing these goals:

• When you hear a teacher make a cynical remark, consider saying, "That almost sounded cynical. You might give others the wrong idea about you." Keeping your tone friendly makes a defensive reaction less likely but still conveys that you don't want cynicism to be a part of your dialogue.

• Approach a teacher you believe to be cynical and ask him or her for help with a particular lesson or student. Say, "I have a problem and you are so good with this type of situation. Can you help me?" It is hard to remain cynical when you help others.

• When you get discouraged, find inspiration in the arts, from friends, or in support groups. I have a few favorite songs that have helped me get through tough times for decades. My favorite "keep me going" song is "It Be's That Way Sometimes" by Nina Simone. She sings, "Don't let the problems of this world drive you slowly out of your mind/Just look at the problem and say, 'It be's that way sometimes.'" She expresses better than I ever could that things are sometimes good, sometimes bad. It's all part of life's cycle. We all have a movie, song, book, poem, or saying that helps us get through difficult periods.

Why not help each of your students find a "comfort song" (or book, or poem, or saying)? Listen to one or two of the songs each week and have the students explain why the songs they chose give them comfort. You can also build a "comfort library" in your classroom with student-designed and -created art, including posters, songs, poems, or stories. When things get tense either academically or behaviorally, ask the students to take a break and listen to their songs or visit the "library" before going back to try to solve the problem. Brainstorm with the class on how turning to comfort songs or art can help them at home when things get difficult.

Believe in Students

One way to build hope in students is to believe in them. That belief, however, must be genuine. Telling them you believe in them will build hope only if it's true. Urban students often hear from teachers about how successful they can be. Unfortunately, many of these teachers are simply going through the motions; they don't truly believe their students can succeed, and this insincerity is not lost on urban children. Their antennae are up for such hypocrisy, and it makes them even more cynical. Believing in students, especially when they make it hard for us to do so, is vitally important.

Many years ago, I made a presentation at a city school in Southern California. During the lunch break, I walked with the principal to the school cafeteria. Our conversation turned serious when he said, "I love everything you said this morning, but it's not practical." This is a hot button for me and I replied, rather heatedly, "You are confusing being practical with being easy. Lots of programs are easy, but not practical, because they don't work. It's never easy to change student behavior. One way you know it's practical is that it is real, not easy."

He pointed to a young lady eating alone and said, "Well, what do you think your ideas will do for her?" The girl, who I later found out was named Roxanne, had recently returned to school from federal prison. She sported spiked, purple-and-orange hair and heavy black makeup—eyes, lips, even her cheeks were painted a dark soot color. Her clothes were revealing, displaying several tattoos, and her body was filled with painful-looking piercings. This was long before such affectations had become fashionable in the mainstream. In short, she was frightening.

I asked the principal what he would do that was "practical." He said he would draw a line and tell her not to cross it. I responded, "What if she said, 'I'll kill you'? Who is more afraid? You drawing your lines, or her threatening to kill you?" Given her history, she is not going to be afraid of his threat. If anything, he might be more afraid of *her* threat. He asked me what I would do and I said I would talk to her, to which he replied, "Go ahead. I'd like to see that."

Dressed in a suit and tie, I sat down at Roxanne's table and said, "Hello." She responded, "Who the fuck are you, asshole?" Relying on my instincts, I drew on two generally effective strategies for interacting with troubled students: meeting the student's needs and challenging the student. Her need to be noticed was obvious, so I started with that.

"My name is Rick, and I'm writing a book about tough kids. You look like you're tough, but I've been fooled before. If you're brave enough to answer a couple of questions, I'll put your name in my book." After some rough banter, she agreed to honestly answer a few questions. "Have you ever had a teacher whom you listened to, did what she wanted, respected her, and learned from her? If so, what made that teacher different from all the others you have had?" I asked. After criticizing my question, she started to cry, the tears streaking her makeup. Her answer brought tears to my eyes, too.

"Those teachers are stupid," she said. "They tell me stupid things like, some-day, I can still go to college, or get a decent job, or be a mother—different from the horrible one I got. Mister, I ain't goin' to no college. I ain't never gonna get a job or be a mother. I'm a dead girl. In prison, if they write your name on the wall, they kill you. My name is on that wall, and I know I'm goin' back there. Every day I wait for the federal marshals to take me back. But those stupid teachers believe in me, and man, it really, really matters."

I hope Roxanne sees her name in print, but I have no idea what happened to her, and her school doesn't, either.

Years ago, I took an informal survey of students who were considered by their schools' administrators and teachers to be the most hopeless. I visited several city campuses around the United States and asked these students what qualities made their favorite teachers so good. "They believe in me" was among the most common answers. Believing in students means that you believe they can succeed in school and, more important, that they can succeed in life.

Accomplishment

Another way to look at hope is through the lens of accomplishment. Accomplishment gives students hope for future successes. If I am able to do something once, I know I can do something else that is similar and perhaps even a little more difficult. A student who has mastered addition, for example, can be confident that he can master division. In urban schools, however, the emphasis on fear of failure and, often, the acceptance of failure lead to a lack of confidence, which in turn leads to hopelessness.

Accomplishment is a great avenue to confidence, but not all accomplishment has the same value when it comes to creating hope (Weiner, 1974). The main determiner in assessing the value of an accomplishment is how the activity was completed. If a student succeeds because she cheated, the task was too simple, she received a great deal of assistance, or she just got lucky, the value of the success is significantly lessened and so, too, is the development of hope. As we discussed in Chapter 3, success without challenge does not foster a sense of pride or achievement, nor does it foster hope.

Degree of Difficulty

Think back to a time when you played a board game with a young child. If you won, were you thrilled? Of course not. Besting a 4-year-old is not a challenge. Now compare that feeling with a time when you beat an older brother or sister or a parent at a game for the very first time. Much different, right?

Psychologist Mihaly Csikszentmihalyi (1990) famously talks about the concept of "flow," a state of utter absorption in the task at hand—what is commonly called "being in the zone." Flow is characterized by a sense of engagement and fulfillment. To achieve a flow state, a balance must be struck between the challenge of the task and the skill of the performer. If the task is too easy or too difficult, flow cannot occur.

Giving students work that is too hard prevents them from achieving the state of flow that Csikszentmihalyi refers to. When the degree of difficulty is too great, frustration sets in. Students should never be forced to do anything that is beyond their ability. The ensuing failure is a result of a poor choice of task on the part of the teacher, not the students' lack of effort. What more can students do but try their best? Even more dangerous, however, is giving students work that is too easy. It sends the message that you do not believe in them and sets them up for severe humiliation if they fail.

Finding a balance between the degree of challenge and the degree of skill is crucial for allowing students to "get into the zone." This combination requires effort, gives great satisfaction in success and little shame in failure, and indicates that you believe in students. Children who play video games are bored to tears with games that are too easy, but they give up rather quickly if the game is too complicated. Neither motivates them to continue playing. When children can choose their level of difficulty, they tend to gravitate toward games that are difficult but possible to win with a high degree of effort. Success at one game level leads to a new, more difficult level of challenge. School tasks can be set up the same way.

Challenge Sheets

One way to make sure students are getting the appropriate level of challenge is to design an assignment with various degrees of difficulty, from easy to very difficult, and let students decide which level is right for them. I call these challenge sheets.

At first glance, challenge sheets look a lot like those boring, tedious worksheets that students dread. The difference is in the challenge. Because students are choosing and trying to meet their own goals, challenge sheets come across more as a game than as an assignment. The seven appendixes at the back of this book provide examples of challenge sheets from various subjects and grades that have been proven to motivate.

At first, many students choose easy goals, but over time the boredom of meeting those goals with little or no effort and the lack of penalty for failing to reach goals creates a need to choose more challenging tasks. Note that there can be no reward for success or penalty for failure with challenge sheets, or else students will not venture out into difficult areas. The stakes must be kept low for this strategy to work. Remember, the goal is to increase learning, build confidence, and show that you believe in students' ability to accomplish challenging tasks. No further incentive is necessary.

Be More Stubborn Than They Are

My longtime friend and colleague Al Mendler frequently says about students, "We must be more stubborn about not giving up on them than they are about making us want to." This is especially important for urban youth. So many of them have experienced failure in school that they have found a comfort zone there. "I cannot fail if I just don't try," they believe. Ramon, an 8th grade student from Chicago, when asked why he never seems to try in school, replied, "It's easier that way." When asked a similar question, Suzette, a junior from Montgomery, Alabama, said, "I can never be disappointed that way."

The Terminator technique discussed in Chapter 2 demonstrates the kind of resolute persistence we must apply to reluctant learners. We must continually say things like the following to students who have given up:

- "I know other teachers have given up on you, but I never will."
- "I'm going to ask you every day how hard you tried, because I refuse to believe that you have totally given up."
- "If you think *you're* stubborn, wait till you see how stubborn *I* can be."
- "I'm going to make it harder for you to fail than for you to give up."

Show Them the Doors

Marybelle visited her high school senior English teacher a year after graduation. "Thank you," she said. "You told me I was the most stubborn student you ever had, and if I used that stubbornness to succeed at something, nothing could hold me back. I thought about that all summer and decided to enroll in City College and not quit until I made it to a four-year college. You were right."

Urban students possess a number of skills necessary for surviving an inner-city existence that can translate into positive and practical applications. For example, the head of a gang might have exceptional leadership skills. The class clown might exhibit interpersonal relationship skills that could be useful in a sales position. Students might have real artistic or musical abilities they don't often get to demonstrate. A teacher who believes in students can offer them hope by helping them identify their strengths and showing them how to use those strengths to open doors they weren't aware existed.

First, make a list of students you believe have feelings of hopelessness. Then identify two or three attributes each student possesses. It doesn't matter whether the attributes are positive or negative. What does matter is how strongly the student exhibits them. With the help of a colleague or two, think about how the attributes could be applied productively. Try to think about how the student might use them to capitalize on career opportunities. Have a private discussion with the student about what you've come up with. If you or your colleagues know prior students with similar attributes who have found ways to parlay them into career opportunities, see if they would be willing to come in and talk to your current student.

Here is one possible exchange between a teacher and student:

Teacher: I've noticed that you are very clever at making jokes. Sometimes they embarrass me or upset me, but they are always funny and have some truth to them.

Student: So?

Teacher: Have you noticed that almost everyone laughs when you tell one of those jokes?

Student: Yeah, they do.

Teacher: I bet if you stopped embarrassing people, those jokes could help you relate to people in business. You could really go far with your humor and insights. Let's try this in class. Tell a few jokes every day if you want, but try not to hurt the other students' or my feelings. At the end of each week, I'll tell you how you are doing.

The Cost of Technology

Any book that covers the realm of education must include a discussion of technology. Just in the time since I started this project, technology has changed radically. Both my cell phone and my MP3 player have become obsolete. For better or worse, I can connect with people I haven't seen in years via social networking sites. Texting has replaced conversation. Tweeting allows for the dissemination of information to thousands instantaneously. By the time this book is in your hands, who knows what benefits technology will have brought us? For the purposes of this book, however, I prefer to look at the other side of the picture. What has technology's ubiquity cost us? For all the positives of technology, it has also profoundly affected the behavior and motivation of children. Kids don't go outside to play the way they used to. For many, "playing a sport" involves a video game console and a controller. Conversation has been greatly reduced, along with social skills. Kids talk more in class out of need more than from a lack of manners. Students are easily bored by the slow pace of learning. As with everything else in life, benefits seldom come without costs, and the benefits of technology come with a hefty price tag.

The greatest hole created by all our dazzling technology is in one-on-one relationships. Teachers can fill this chasm. We can talk to students and listen to what they say. We can put an arm around them. We can offer high fives for successes. We can, in short, care about them. The relationships we forge with our students can provide a consistency and immediacy that technology cannot touch. Kids like it faster, but learn better slower. We can encourage, support, appreciate, and care about students in ways that only humans can. We can do what no technological device can: believe in them and, in so doing, foster hope.

6

Welcoming All Students to School and Class

Imagine being Chuck, a 3rd grader from New York City's South Bronx. When he goes into the corner convenience store to buy a candy bar, the owner says, "I'm watching you. Don't you dare put anything in your pocket." On the way home from school, he must navigate carefully so he doesn't end up on a street controlled by a gang. When he finally arrives home, his mother doesn't ask him how his day went. Instead, she demands, "It's about time you got home. Watch your little sister. I'm going out."

School can and should be a respite for students—a safe, friendly place. Schools should welcome all students, regardless of how they behave or how well they do academically. Unwelcome students are unmotivated students.

Students are far more likely to want to learn when they connect emotionally, psychologically, and intellectually with school. Every educator knows that a student will learn more if she wants to come to class than if she does not. The difficulty lies in finding out how to reach the most resistant and disconnected learners. Unfortunately, the most effective methods of welcoming are also the most alien to the culture of the typical school. Schools must change significantly, even drastically, to be successful. The following six principles are guides to these changes:

- Schools are for all children, not just the ones who behave well and get high grades.
- Learning something (even a little something) is better than learning nothing.
- Any procedure that helps "good" students get better and "bad" students get worse has no place in a school.
- Students need to be part of something bigger than themselves.
- To get better at something, students need an opportunity to do it.
- Assisting others helps students heal emotionally.

Let's examine how these principles can be put into practice.

Providing Opportunity

Ask yourself if the following scenarios make sense:

- A baseball coach says to a player, "You dropped too many balls in the last game. You are forbidden to practice until you get better."
- A math teacher says to a student, "You are very poor at computation; until you improve, you are not allowed to do any math."
- A drama teacher tells a student, "You messed up those lines. Until you master them, you cannot rehearse them at all."

Clearly, adhering to such practices would be ridiculous. How can players improve without practice, math students learn without doing math, or drama students deliver lines effectively without rehearsal? They cannot. Yet we say similar things to students all the time, with the same dismal results. Do any of the following sound familiar?

- You misbehaved on the last field trip; you can't go on any more trips until you prove that you have learned how to behave.
- That's not the way we behave on a playground; line up against the wall. You can't play with your friends until you learn how to behave.
- On Friday we are having a pizza party for those who completed their work. You didn't complete yours, so you can't come.
- You! Out of class. Don't come back until you learn how to behave.

If the only way to learn a new behavior is to practice it, why do we habitually exclude the least skilled students from opportunities to practice the behaviors they need to master and provide already-proficient students with the most opportunities? Should it not be the other way around? Most schools offer extracurricular activities as an incentive for children to try harder and withhold such activities as a punishment for inappropriate behavior. Both strategies often fail because they neither encourage good behavior nor increase academic or behavioral motivation in those who need it the most.

For example, imagine you are a student the same age as those you presently teach. Your class is offered a pizza party, an exciting field trip, or some other special opportunity for those who have reached an academic or behavioral goal. You are told you cannot participate because you didn't earn it. Would you say, "That sounds great! I'll try harder next time to earn it!" or "That sounds stupid. I'm glad I don't have to go!"? Not surprisingly, most students who are denied such opportunities respond negatively, usually denigrating the opportunity. As with many other situations in their lives, they've learned that it hurts less to decide they don't want something they can't have. Or they feel that it is better to be in control of the situation; it is better to tell the teacher they don't want something than to be told they can't have it.

It is true that successful students may work harder to earn the incentive being offered, but they are already motivated, so the benefit of the external reward is minimal. In addition, incentives may occasionally work with unsuccessful students, but they almost never work with the least motivated students or with those with a history of exclusion who have accepted that outcome. In short, offering extracurricular activities as an incentive works best for the students who need it the least and works worst for the students who need it the most. And withholding those opportunities as a punishment does nothing to bolster struggling students' motivation.

Something Bigger Than Ourselves

Growing up I felt part of something bigger than myself; I was part of a family. Being part of a family meant I was protected, loved, and cared for. I was taught, coached, played with, and teased. But I also had responsibilities. I could not shame, embarrass, or humiliate my family. I had to live by its values. Many times I had to compromise. I didn't always get what I wanted. But there was nothing I could ever do, no matter how bad, that would stop my family from loving me or believing in me. I always knew that they loved me unconditionally.

One key to giving students hope and fostering motivation is to accept and welcome them in this same way—unconditionally. The school can become for students something bigger than themselves, something that they can feel a part of. Yvette, a high school student from Jackson, Mississippi, hated school and counted the days until she could drop out. A friend told her she should try out for the girls' basketball team. The principal of Yvette's school was wise enough to understand that even though her grades didn't qualify her to play varsity sports, joining the team might turn her attitude around. He was right. Yvette not only made the team but also became one of its best players. Soon, she couldn't wait to come to school. She improved her grades enough to enroll in a junior college and planned to attend a four-year school on an athletic scholarship. Finding a positive, affirming connection to school changed her life. Had Yvette's principal adhered strictly to the rules, he would have kept her from the very thing that ended up providing the motivation she so desperately needed.

All this is not to say that students don't need consequences for misbehavior. Trying to provide unconditional acceptance and a place where students can feel safe and included doesn't mean there are no consequences for unacceptable behavior. Removal and denial of opportunity, however, are not consequences but rather punishments imposed by the school or teacher, and, as we've already discussed, punishment is seldom an effective motivator. Although they are sometimes necessary, they should never be at the top of the list of preferred strategies.

Sometimes, we must ask students to leave our classrooms. How we do this is more important than the fact that we are doing it. Couples, parents and children, and friends all sometimes need time apart. Teachers, too, need time apart from some students. Temporary time-outs or classroom removals are occasionally necessary as a means to teach more effectively or just to mentally get through the day. There is a difference, however, between a short separation and sending the message that students need to earn the right to be in a class. Note the different messages implied in the following examples:

- "OUT!! Don't come back until you're ready to learn."
- "We need a break from each other before this situation gets worse. I hope it's not for too long."

Strategies

The three main concerns when including students in learning or extracurricular opportunities, be they field trips, dances, sports, playground privileges, assemblies, or any other school functions, are (1) fostering a positive attitude in the students so that they want to behave and are motivated to learn; (2) teaching the students the skills they need to be successful; and (3) providing a safe environment for others.

Foster a positive attitude in students. Most educators believe that if a child earns an opportunity, he or she will value it more. In addition, the child's desire to earn the opportunity will result in appropriate behavior. Students with expectations for success may be motivated to earn extracurricular activities or special benefits, but the more a student expects failure, the less effective this strategy is. Students with low expectations for success may purposely misbehave and thus lose out on the opportunity being offered so that they can feel in control. A better solution, although it may sound counterintuitive, is to include them regardless of what they have done or not done. Although punishment for certain behaviors may be necessary, exclusion can lead to a worsening of motivation, which ultimately leads to further undesirable behavior. We hope instead to create the feeling in the student that disappointing others is worse than punishment. When talking to a student you might previously have excluded from an extracurricular activity, speak to him or her in private, offering some kind, inclusive words—and make sure you mean what you are saying. Troubled kids are attuned to hypocrisy and will shut down if they sense a lack of sincerity. If you're having trouble thinking of some nice words that you truly believe, find a reason to believe them. For example, you probably really do want the student to improve, and you can probably think of some good that will come out of the student joining the rest of the group. Here is an example of what you might say. I have left out the student's response for the sake of clarity, but in reality, he or she will usually have something to say:

We are going on a field trip next week, and I have given a lot of thought to whether or not you should come, given what happened the last time. I have decided that you can go, not only on this trip, but on any trip the class takes. You will be included in everything this class does because you are part of the class. Besides, if you didn't come, I'd miss you. You always make me laugh, and I love that. And I know you'll never admit it, but you'd miss us, too. If you misbehave again, there will be a consequence, but you won't be excluded.

If you heard something like this, would you want to try harder or less hard?

Teach students skills they need to succeed. If students lack the skills needed to perform, merely offering prized activities won't change anything. We must teach them what they need to know. This is especially true of social skills. So many urban children's parents work long hours, frequently at multiple jobs, with little time left over to teach social skills. And, in some cases, parents are simply not emotionally present in their children's lives. These students should not be left out of school learning opportunities because their parents were less instructive than others. It doesn't help to punish them twice for having ineffective or overworked parents.

Make a list of the behaviors that concern you about the target students and take the time to teach them how to correct those behaviors in a nonpunitive manner. Remember that simply telling students what behaviors they need to change is not enough. You must also tell them how to change. For example, simply telling a student not to fight is a "what," whereas giving students strategies for dealing with their anger is a "how." Both are necessary.

Students may understand that hitting others is inappropriate but not know how to avoid it without instruction and practice. Teaching social skills is like teaching sports, drama, or academic skills. It involves explaining the skills, modeling the skills, and providing opportunities for lots of practice. Good coaches know that performance cannot change with one practice. Repetition leads to maximum performance. Nothing less is required for social skills. Often, the impetus for the undesirable behavior is understandable. It is understandable, for example, that a student who believes he has been insulted would want to defend himself. You can open the dialogue with this student by acknowledging the validity of that impulse before critiquing the resulting behavior:

One thing I like about you is that you defend yourself. You never let anyone insult you or your family. I admire that. But you can't do it by hitting. There are better ways to defend your honor, and I will teach them to you. Then you can help me teach them to the rest of the class.

Provide a safe environment for others. There are risks to including troubled students in learning and extracurricular opportunities. They may present danger to other students, school officials, or people in the community. We can counter this threat by carefully teaming the target student with adults, older students, or my favorite, senior citizens. Every community has assisted-living communities with older people who are healthy enough to come to school for an hour or two. These people have a wide range of skills they can share with a generation eager to interact with them. They can act as chaperones on field trips, as tutors, and as mentors. They can play with younger children on the playground and offer life and career advice to older children.

Troubled youth seem to change miraculously in the company of senior citizens. Those who have seen such interaction report that troubled youth often relate better to the elderly than to their more responsible classmates. But both parties benefit greatly from the connection. Adding meaningful activities to seniors' lives helps them live longer and more happily, especially if they are lonely. Of course, not all seniors are good companions or mentors for children. Predators grow old, too. Be sure to exercise the same cautions you would when asking any adult to interact with students.

The Altruism Consequence

Another option for providing a safe environment for all students and faculty serves a double purpose. I said earlier that misbehavior requires a consequence. My favorite method for addressing undesirable behavior has the benefit of motivating students, helping them heal their pain, and making them feel welcome in the school or classroom, all at the same time. I call it the *altruism consequence*. When students misbehave, they "give back" by helping other students in need. Although this may seem more a punishment than a consequence, keep in mind that whereas punishments aim to make students suffer to deter them from future misbehavior, consequences are designed to help students learn to make better choices. A consequence may occur as the natural outcome of a student's choices *or* as a learning situation set up to address the cause of troublesome behavior (rather than the behavior itself). When kids who feel unwelcome help others, they often realize that they are needed and have something to offer, which leads to a greater sense of self-worth.

In most schools, a fight leads to a three- or five-day suspension. This is about as effective as giving bank robbers money. The suspended students get to watch television, play video games, eat junk food, hang out, and generally have fun. Some spend the day texting their friends in class, thereby creating a distraction without even being in school. Instead of sending them home, why not send these students to a lower grade (high school to middle school, middle school to elementary school) to help other troubled students for the duration of the suspension? Tasks might include tutoring, being a bodyguard to students who are being bullied, playground monitoring, partnering on field trips, or lunch room duty. How do you think a troublesome 7th grader would respond to a tough high school junior telling him to watch his behavior?

I have worked with several schools that have tried this process and reaped remarkable results. Students on both sides benefit greatly. Remember, this process is meant to help heal and should never be used as an opportunity to be earned. There are three situations in which this approach works well: as a consequence for misbehavior, as a motivational strategy for unmotivated students who do not misbehave, and as a motivational strategy for high-performing or adequately performing students.

Misbehaving students. Tutoring, field trip partnering, or any of the other aforementioned tasks can replace detention, suspension, behavior plans, or calls home. Many schools that have adopted this approach have converted in-school suspension (ISS) rooms into tutoring labs. Students sent to ISS are teamed with other students who need tutoring help. The ISS time becomes an altruistic opportunity. And because "pain understands pain," troubled youth bond in positive ways. At Fisher Middle School in San Jose, California, for example, I overhead a 7th grade gangbanger who had been paired with a 1st grader tell the younger student not to join a gang because "they aren't as much fun as they look."

A 3rd grader from Flint, Michigan, was nicknamed "the terrorist" because everywhere he went, another student yelled in pain from some injury he had inflicted. We sent this young bully to the 1st grade to help tutor a poor reader.

The 3rd grader could barely read himself and did little classroom work and no homework, but this didn't matter because we had our sights set on a higher goal. The 3rd grader responded very negatively: "I ain't goin' to no 1st grade. You can't make me. You're not the boss of me." We calmly responded, "Actually, we are the boss of you and we can make you go to the 1st grade. We cannot make you tutor, however, so if you prefer, you can just go there and do nothing." Children, and adults for that matter, would rather do almost anything than nothing. This is why you are willing to read a 10-year-old magazine in a doctor's waiting room. After a day or two, the 3rd grader asked if he could begin tutoring.

In about a week, the 1st grade class cheered when the 3rd grader appeared at the door. He started combing his hair and straightening his shirt before going into the classroom. He even asked his 3rd grade teacher to help him figure out ways to get his "student" to do homework. Meanwhile, his own grades gradually improved. The biggest improvement, however, was on the social skills front: he stopped hurting other students.

This strategy would have failed if the student had had to earn the privilege of tutoring or if an improvement in his behavior had ended his tutoring "sentence." Helping someone else healed some of the wounds that led him to hurt others. Imagine the principal's surprise when our former terror asked, after his 1st grade tutee got sick and had to miss two weeks of school, if he could go to the younger student's house to help him, explaining, "I'll get all caught up on my work, but he really needs me." Countless victims of war, natural disasters, and serious illness have been able to heal their emotional wounds by offering aid to others going through similar experiences. This scenario is no different.

One of the concerns I have heard about moving troubled students into other classes is the fear that the receiving teacher will then have one more problem child in her class. But as our reformed 3rd grader's situation demonstrates, in reality, the opposite is true. Because the helping student spends time with one of that teacher's own problem students, she has one less problem to worry about. Everyone wins.

Unmotivated students who do not misbehave. Students who show up for class but do nothing while they are there can only benefit from being sent to another class two or three times a week to help younger or disabled students.

One of the best ways to learn a subject is to teach it to others, so the older students can help the younger students in whatever class they left (e.g., if they weren't doing anything in their math class, they can be sent to help another student with math). The bonding of a younger and an older student increases both students' motivation to learn.

High-performing or adequately performing students. One of the fears regarding this strategy is based on the belief that it is wrong to reward misbehavior. I've had teachers ask me, "If the only way to become a helper is to be bad, then won't good kids be bad in order to get to do it?" There is a ring of truth to this claim, but the problem can be overcome by allowing any student to be a helper if he or she chooses. In the same way that troubled youth should not be excluded from learning and extracurricular opportunities, neither should well-behaved, high-performing kids be excluded from special opportunities.

One additional benefit of the altruism consequence is that it teaches the value of helping others. Schools are designed primarily to help individuals in a selfish manner, ideally preparing them to succeed at college, in the workplace, and in life. I love the idea that success in this instance means helping others as well as ourselves. In the course of a recent conversation I had with Dwight Allen, Dwight observed that "the richness of life is the service we can do for others. That's one of the great secrets of creation."

Welcome Students, Make a Difference

You can do many things in the course of a day to make students feel welcome. Try greeting troubled students personally on as many days as possible. Ask them how their night went. Comment on a sports event or play they participated in. Wish them a great class. Tell them you're glad they came to school today. Ask them if there is anything special you can do to help them be successful.

Ask your students to think about the best teacher they've ever had. Let them write or say what that teacher did that made them a favorite. Ask them to think about what that teacher did that helped them enjoy the class. Use as many of their responses as possible, especially with your most difficult students. If a student does not have a favorite teacher, ask him or her to tell you what he or she thinks a teacher would need to do to become a favorite.

The more students feel welcome and like an integral part of the school or class, the less likely they are to misbehave, and the more likely they are to learn. The ideas presented in this chapter are not quick fixes. They require commitment. In the long run, however, they are worth the work required to implement them, because it is always easier to teach kids who are invested in their academic progress and environment than it is to teach those who are not.

7

Building Motivating Lessons

Once students have developed positive attitudes about the school or classroom, we need to design lessons that involve, stimulate, excite, illuminate, and create a desire to learn. How many times have you had a TV news program on in the background, only to be hooked by a news story that drew your attention? Great lessons compel students to pay attention in the same way. When students are actively engaged and challenged and have their natural sense of curiosity tweaked, motivation is greatly enhanced. Here are some ways your lessons can "hook" students.

Create a Dynamic Opening

If you live with other people, how long does it generally take you to figure out when they are in a bad mood? Hours, minutes, or seconds? Have you ever seen a child watching television with a remote control in his hand? How long does it take that child to change the station if he is bored? Hours, minutes, or seconds? Students come into classrooms and determine whether or not they will like a class within the first few minutes. As my friend Mark Phillips of San Francisco State University says, "They have a remote control in their minds with three buttons: on, off, and disrupt."

In elementary grades, this applies each time you change the lesson. The first five minutes of instruction can determine the attitude of students, especially troubled ones, for the remainder of the class. Your opening works best when it gets students to think, "Today's going to be fun."

The activities that teachers typically start class with—taking attendance, handing out papers, collecting papers—are best done after class has already gotten off to a good start. If any of these activities must be done at the beginning of class, try having a student do them while you start the lesson with something more engaging. Never start class with, "OK, class, open your books to page X." You might as well invite your students to take a nap.

Use Teasers

Teasers are a great way to perk up students' ears and engage their curiosity about what is coming next. I learned the effectiveness of teasers while watching the news. The anchor always says, "Coming up next. . . ." and if we are sufficiently curious, we stay tuned through three commercials and two other stories to find out what the teaser promises. Here are two teasers, one for English and one for math, that illustrate the strategy:

- *English:* Which of the following would get students more excited about their next English class: "Tomorrow, we are going to start a unit on William Shakespeare. Please read the first act of *As You Like It*," or "Tomorrow, we are going to see how William Shakespeare's play *As You Like It* is sexier than an episode of *Desperate Housewives*"?
- *Math:* Which of the following would get students more excited about their next math class: "Tomorrow we are going to study functions. Please do this worksheet tonight," or "Tomorrow we are going to see how functions are used in the development of video games. Then we are going to create our own video game to share with the rest of the school"?

It is initially hard to think of good teasers, but once you get in the habit of using them, they become a natural part of your repertoire. In order to work effectively, teasers must appeal to the least motivated students in class. This requires that you know enough about their interests to make a compelling connection to the upcoming content. Further, you must deliver on the teaser or students will no longer listen to you. If you say you will discuss how *As You Like It* is sexier than an episode of *Desperate Housewives*, then do it and do it early in the lesson. Likewise, if you say you are going to create a video game, then create one.

Connect Songs to Content

Divide the class into small groups and ask each group to make a list of the members' favorite songs. Require or strongly suggest writing the name of the song if they know it. Consensus is not required; it is more important to make as long a list as possible. When the lists are completed, ask the students to connect one song title from the list in some way with the topic to be learned. You will be amazed at what your students come up with, and connecting something they love with something to be learned is a positive, engaging way to begin any lesson. Another way to do this activity is to tell students in advance what the topic is and have them bring song ideas to class.

I've come up with my own list of songs. I thought about using songs that are popular today, but by the time this book comes out, new songs will almost certainly have replaced the ones I would have chosen, so I simply chose songs that are relevant to me. The songs your students think of will be popular at the time and will be relevant to them:

- *Astronomy:* "Stairway to Heaven"
- *Biology:* "Every Breath You Take"
- *Art:* "Purple Haze"
- *Driver Education:* "Running on Empty"
- *Geography:* "Wish You Were Here"
- *Current Events/Environmental Studies:* "What's Going On"
- *Math:* "Three Times a Lady"
- *History:* "The Way We Were"

Cultivate a "Need to Know" Mentality

Great questions drive great lessons. A great question gets under students' skin so that they are compelled by curiosity to find the answer. Here are samples from various content areas that teachers have shared with me:

- *Middle school math:* What does Martin Luther King have in common with algebra? Answer: They both are concerned with equality.
- *1st grade science lesson on particles:* What is the smallest thing you've ever held in your hand?
- *Upper-level history class studying the pilgrims:* Is there anything your parents could ever do to you that would make you run away from home?
- *Elementary school art:* If humans could be a color other than any of the colors they already are, what color would they be? Why do you think this? Draw some people of this color.
- *Math, all levels:* How can four people play a video game designed for two players?
- *High school English:* If *Hamlet* were a television sitcom, what would be a better name for it?
- *Elementary school English:* What is the best name for a book about your life? Why do *fuse* and *choose* rhyme, but *choose* and *goose* do not?
- *High school social studies:* If Napoleon spread nationalism, how did nationalism bring him down?
- *Geography:* Why does Israel have more fertile soil than other Middle Eastern countries that share the same desert?
- *High school biology:* If women are the only gender that can lactate, why do men have nipples?
- *2nd grade reading:* We are going to redesign the alphabet. What three letters can be eliminated?
- *8th grade physical education:* Why is a soccer ball harder to control in the gym than on grass?
- *Middle school English:* Why don't *good* and *food* rhyme? Given the definition of *best*, can you have more than one best friend?
- *Psychology:* Did Pavlov salivate along with his dogs when he heard a bell ring?
- *High school physical education:* In a championship game, is it better for a coach to say, "Even if you lose, I'm very proud of you" or "You'd better play your best, because if you lose, you are nothing"?
- *Elementary science:* If your blood is red, then why are your veins blue?

- *Middle school art:* How does the word *cadaver* relate to Leonardo da Vinci?[1]

Let Students Create Questions

Students are great at thinking of their own compelling questions about a subject. After giving them some sample questions of your own, ask them to brainstorm as many questions as they can in a controlled time span. Ten minutes usually works well. Let students answer questions other than their own in a class discussion or in groups.

Encourage Students to Find the Answers Themselves

Most lessons begin with answers in the form of content that is lectured on, discussed, read, or described in some way, followed by questions in the form of a test, quiz, or discussion. This is an unnatural way of sequencing. In the normal course of events, questions come before answers. Questions, in fact, create the need for answers. Have you ever bought software for your computer? Did you study the user manual before you inserted the installation disk? Most people don't unless they have a question. When you bought your last car, did you read the owner's manual before driving off the lot? Probably not. We generally don't care about answers unless they provide information about a question we already have. The same is true for great lessons that motivate. All students

---

1. *Teacher's note:* I was teaching my students about realism shading. I wrote this question on the chalkboard: How does the word cadaver relate to Leonardo da Vinci? My 9th graders saw this question in passing and were very curious. Some of the students did not know what a cadaver was, so first they had to figure that out. When I asked them what they knew about the artist, they answered, "He painted the *Mona Lisa*." I acknowledged their answer and said, "Yes, but there is so much more that he is famous for!" Once everyone knew what a cadaver was, I proceeded to tell the students how da Vinci used cadavers as models to create accurate medical drawings for doctors. He drew the organs, bones, tendons, and muscles. They were so grossed out and I loved it! (Lorijean Wallence, art teacher, Wilson Central Junior High, West Lawn, Pennsylvania)

have a natural desire to understand the puzzling world around them. By starting lessons with great questions before presenting answers, we tap into students' sense of curiosity and create the desire to learn. Learning becomes even more powerful when students find the answers to questions for themselves individually, in pairs, or in small groups.

Encourage Students to Guess

Almost every subject area has its own specialized word that means guessing— for example, hypothesizing, estimating, inferring, foreshadowing, and predicting. If a student ever responds to a question with "I don't know" or something similar, ask the student to guess the answer. Once a student has guessed, even wildly, she has a vested interest in seeing how close she came to being right. Have you ever taken a quiz in a magazine and *not* looked at the answer key on another page to see if you were right? The same psychology holds true for the learning process. When I taught 7th grade, about twice a month I would tell my students that they had no homework on a particular night; all they had to do was guess at the answers. In fact, I forbade them from doing any actual work. (Amusingly, many students "cheated" and actually did their work.) The next day, they were very curious to see how close their guesses came to the real answers.

Pose questions to students and have them guess at the answers throughout your lesson. You can have students guess individually, in pairs, or in small groups. Here are some of my favorite examples:

- *Science:* Hold up a strange object or point out a chemical reaction and ask students to guess what it is used for.
- *Math:* Ask whether students would prefer to receive one million dollars upfront or to receive one penny the first day of the month and then to double the amount every day for the entire month.
- *Social studies:* Provide lesser-known facts about famous historical figures and have students guess to whom they refer. Younger students can be given multiple choices.
- *Art:* Have students guess which color fits best in an incomplete picture.
- *Literature:* Adapt the social studies example to a book's characters. Have students guess at alternative endings for short stories.

- *Music:* Play part of a song and have students guess the next few notes.
- *Psychology:* Have students guess the mental illness based on a few symptoms.
- *Physical Education:* Have students guess what rule is not legitimate in a given game about to be played.

Offer Real Choices

Choices give students a feeling of control over the lesson and over the evaluation of their performance. For those students with control issues or a strong need for more control over their lives, having choices can effectively boost motivation. When assigning homework or class projects, picking reading material, or composing quiz and test questions, keep in mind that the more choices students have, the more likely they are to find something that they can connect with and that will motivate them.

Be sure to give enough variety and quantity of choices. Letting students choose any 14 homework problems out of 15 is not a real choice. Make sure the ratio is at least one-third to one-half; for example, allowing students to choose 10 out of 15 questions is adequate. For a highly motivational option, invite students to create their own alternatives, be they test questions, projects, or in-class activities.

Offering choices as a part of quizzes or tests has three great benefits. First is the sense of student control and empowerment I've already mentioned. Second is that students end up answering all the questions anyway. How else can they decide on which to officially answer on the test? Third, and perhaps the best benefit for the teacher, is the dramatic decrease in the amount of correcting. If students only have to answer half of the questions on a test, that's a 50 percent decrease in the answers that need to be read, evaluated, and commented on. For many teachers, that's like getting a second life.

Use Evaluation Diagnostically

At the conclusion of the learning activity, students need to feel that they have mastered the task at hand, or at least improved. They should be able to do something, understand something, distinguish something, or comprehend something better than they did before the lesson. If they cannot, then the teacher needs to assess what additional instruction is needed. Finding out how to improve a student's score is more useful than simply grading the result and handing it back with no follow-up. If a student gets a math problem wrong, for example, it is difficult to design a remedy without knowing whether the mistake was the result of carelessness, a simple reading error, or a true lack of understanding of how to perform the calculation.

When students see that they can improve, they are motivated to continue. But the contrary is also true. When students do not improve after an instructional sequence, they lose hope and motivation decreases. As we previously discussed, however, it is important not to assign students tasks that are too easy. No pride or sense of accomplishment comes from successfully completing a task that is below students' level of competence. It is far better to teach students the skills needed for challenging tasks than to guarantee success with tasks that are too easy.

Below I've included 22 activities that can turbocharge any lesson to make it more stimulating, exciting, engaging, and motivating. A number of teachers have used these activities across a variety of age groups, and all have met with a high degree of success in urban settings, even with the most reluctant of learners.

Identify positive and negative teacher characteristics. We've already discussed how helpful it can be to know what students feel they need and don't need from you in the instructional process. This activity asks students to represent those characteristics artistically. Ask your students to think of one of their best teachers, one with whom they've succeeded, and draw a symbol to represent that teacher. For younger students, you can provide symbols like rainbows, smiley faces, and hot air balloons, and let the students pick the one they like best. Ask students to do the same with a teacher with whom they had trouble being successful (while telling them that you don't want them to name any names). Ask students to write under each symbol—or have them discuss—what the teachers did that led to their successes and failures. Make a chart to hang on the wall that lists the things you will and will not do in that class as a result of the activity.

Create a composite "perfect teacher" drawing. Divide the class into groups of three to five students. Provide each group with a large sheet of newsprint or flipchart paper and ask them to draw a composite picture of the perfect teacher. Encourage humor. Tape the pictures up around the room and have a gallery walk for the class. During the walk, have each group explain what it included in its picture and why. Follow the gallery walk with a discussion of what you can do to be like their pictures. An interesting follow-up is to repeat the procedure with drawings of the perfect student.

Discuss allegories. Tell students a compelling story and have them answer a difficult question at the end. Then ask them to compare their real-life behavior with their answers and see if they match. The process of extrapolating the elements of the story to their own lives and decisions leads to fruitful discussion.

For example, I learned the following allegory from Dwight Allen and use it in seminars with great success. It has many possible discussion points and relates directly to the content of this book. I begin by presenting the following scenario: "If you struggled greatly to climb a mountain and felt great pride in achieving the goal of reaching the top and then discovered an escalator on the other side of the mountain, would you tell a friend who wanted to climb the same mountain about the escalator? Why or why not?" I then ask, "Which student is more valued, the one who tries hard but manages to climb only halfway up the mountain, or the one who gets to the top by using the escalator?" Finally, I ask, "Who gets an *A*: a student who tries hard and gets 50 percent, or one who doesn't try at all but gets 95 percent?"

Legitimize answers. Influential U.S. educator Madeline Hunter recommended that when students give wrong answers, educators should acknowledge the part that is right before correcting the part that is wrong. For example, if you asked the class to identify the first president of the United States, and a student answered, "Abraham Lincoln," you might respond, "You're right that he was a U.S. president, but he wasn't the first."

Students are more encouraged to get involved in class discussions when their answers are appreciated. I do believe that there are limits to legitimizing answers, however. If the student answered "Mick Jagger," for example, I wouldn't say, "He is male, as all U.S. presidents have been." I might instead make a joke and insert a factoid: "He'd probably get the most votes if he could run, but a British citizen cannot be president of the United States. Does anyone have an opinion about that law?" The more we value and appreciate students' answers, the more likely it is that every student will want to participate.

Plan. Planning is crucial for developing responsibility and is closely linked to motivation. When figuring out how to complete assignments or doing long-term projects, planning is a very useful tool. When students develop their own plans, they are more likely to commit to them. Plans work best when they are detailed and specific. "I will finish my project on time" is not specific enough to help with planning, whereas saying "I will check the Internet for a list of resources, take careful notes, and make a preliminary list of potentially useful sources" lays out specific, concrete actions.

Another fun use of planning is for students to develop imaginary plans for people they are studying. Ask them to consider what the best plan would be for Holden Caulfield, Benjamin Franklin, Marie Curie, or Pablo Picasso, for example. This is a flexible, open-ended activity; the possibilities are endless and depend on the goals of the lesson.

Provide concrete experiences. Mihaly Csikszentmihalyi (1990) has found that concrete experiences are more motivating than open-ended experiences. Thus, students are more motivated when they know how long an assignment will last, especially if it is a routine task. Tell students that the class will work on spelling from 9:15–9:45 a.m., for example, and stick to that schedule. If you've ever attended a seminar where the presenter went over the scheduled speaking time, you probably remember how unmotivated you quickly became to continue listening. Likewise, when airport delays drag out in small, repetitive segments, it's much more frustrating than if you know the total delay time upfront, regardless of how long it is. Students feel the same way about lessons.

Self-evaluate. When it comes to drills, homework, and other routine tasks, motivation and learning increase when students correct and evaluate their own work. Typically, these types of assignments should not be graded or recorded. Self-evaluation is especially effective when students also choose their own level of challenge.

Hold a student "stand-in." During a biology lesson taught by my colleague Larry Quinsland, students could not grasp the way blood flowed through the body and brought oxygen to various organs. Larry solved the problem by using the students themselves to form the cardiovascular system, placing them in a carefully planned configuration. Four students represented each valve of the heart, two others represented the lungs, and other students stood in for various other organs. Students then walked through the "system" exchanging red cards for blue to simulate the way oxygen is exchanged in the body. The same technique can be used for any body or mechanical function you are teaching.

Develop advertisements. I especially like asking students to get together in small groups and develop ads for what they are about to study or for a review of a completed unit. When students develop a positive ad for content they are about to study, they begin the unit with a positive attitude about it. Students can create ads for a nearly endless range of topics, from fractions and the periodic table to Charles Dickens and World War II. These ads can be as simple or as complex as you want and can take however long is appropriate for the unit of study—anywhere from an hour to a week. Most ad presentations run three to seven minutes long and can include a wide variety of elements: posters, jingles, skits, video clips, and computer graphics (e.g., PowerPoint).

Talk to students about different types of ads and give them a choice of what kind of slant they want their ads to take. For example, their ads could use such techniques as persuasion (convincing the audience that your product is best), celebrity endorsement, the bandwagon argument (everybody uses it!), statistics (90 percent of users were satisfied), comparison with a leading competitor, and so on. Students' individual level of involvement in creating the ads can be determined by interest or ability. Some students can sing or act, whereas others excel at graphic design or drawing. Coming up with advertisements creates a lot of positive energy within the classroom; making them will become one of your students' favorite activities.

Host quiz shows. Students love activities modeled after quiz shows. Quiz shows based on television formats make for excellent review and reinforcement of previously covered material. *Family Feud* and *Jeopardy!* both provide great formats on which to base your quiz show activities. I strongly recommend, however, that you do away with one aspect of quiz shows when adapting them for classroom use: elimination for giving wrong answers. Think about spelling bees. These contests eliminate the worst spellers who need the most prac- tice and give the best spellers more opportunity to improve. Take care not to exclude those who most need the practice. I also suggest staying away from having all-boy and all-girl teams. Boys and girls must learn to work together in school, just as they will have to as adults in the workplace.

Although friendly competition can enhance engagement, remember to stress the fun of playing the game rather than emphasizing winning the game. I strongly advise against offering an actual prize to the winning group. Awarding mock points for winning that don't really mean anything aside from providing momentary "bragging rights" is the way to go. All students must enjoy the activity or it will not be motivating for them.

Debate the opposite. Offer students an opinion question, either individually or in groups, and ask them to take a side. Have them write down three or four reasons why they think their opinion is right. Then ask them to argue the opposite point of view. Try to choose issues that are both related to your content and related to something of high interest to the students.

Rotate answers. Class discussion usually turns into a series of one-on-one conversations between the teacher and a student. Once one student is called on, the others tend to stop thinking or paying attention. To minimize this phenomenon, call on other students to comment on the previous student's answer. "Do you agree?" "Can you add more?" "What did he mean by that?" and "What other possibilities are there?" are all good follow-up questions or prompts for continuing the dialogue. Be sure to be persistent about calling on unmotivated students without embarrassing or harassing them. Let them know that they are part of the class and that you expect them to participate.

Connect to hobbies. The more connections you can find between content and the activities students love, the more likely it is that they will enjoy learning about that content. Begin by collecting a list of your students' favorite home activities and hobbies (no sex or drugs, please!). Pick five or six from the list and develop questions about those activities that connect to the lesson. Ask the students to choose which questions they want to answer, either individually or in groups.

Write songs. Students love to write songs in the genre of their choice. Asking them to write songs about curriculum topics is a great way to generate excitement about the topic to be studied. Even some of the most reluctant learners love this activity. Listening to students sing their songs is great fun. Here's an example of one student's song about physics:

> *Don't stop it*
> *You can't stop it*
> *It's inertia*
> *That train that's moving will just keep moving*
> *According to the laws of Sir Isaac Newton*

Way across the ocean
In his first law of motion
He said that an object at rest would stay at rest
And because he could say it best
He had the notion that an object in motion would stay in motion
If an object does persist
It is guaranteed to resist
To change its state of motion
Because inertia will keep it going
But don't tell your mom and pop
That an object will not stop
That is a mistake and like your car has a brake
Friction is the force that you know of course
That will bring that object to rest

Build time machines. Have your students design or even build time machines, individually or in groups. This activity is especially good for younger students but is fun and motivating for all ages. It also incorporates different learning styles and abilities, so is a good activity for students whose mechanical or art skills are better than their writing skills. Once the machines are built, the students can then go backward or forward to another time and write a story, an essay, or an eyewitness account—depending on the subject area—of what they think they might see.

Hold a lightning round. One of the most motivationally useful elements of quiz shows is the "lightning round." The fast pace and tension keep students engaged and excited. What if, instead of a regular review before a test or quiz, we used lightning rounds? The change in name alone invites engagement. Imagine telling students, "We've got a quiz coming up, so tomorrow we are going to have a lightning round to help you prepare. It will be fast, so be ready for speed. Good luck!" That certainly sounds better than saying, "Tomorrow, we are going to review this chapter. It will help you do better on the upcoming quiz." But the lightning round can—and should—be more than just a name change. Structure the review like a real game show lightning round, with teams, fast-paced questions, and no pauses for discussion until the end of the round. Let one team ask the other teams questions based on the content. The goal is to make the experience exciting.

Go on a scavenger hunt. Adults often groan when a scavenger hunt is announced at a party, but kids love them. You can have students hunt for actual items or for virtual items. For the former, make a list of real items related to the content of the lesson and have teams of students search at home or in the school for as many of the items as they can find. Buying or stealing items results in elimination of that category from the activity. Make sure the list includes a range of items from easy-to-find to difficult-but-possible. Another option is to allow students to make some items, such as a replica of the United States Constitution, for example. For a unit on racism in America, a baseball could symbolize Jackie Robinson breaking the color barrier in major league baseball. For a science unit, a stuffed monkey could symbolize the animal trials done during the development of the polio vaccine, or a green plant could represent photosynthesis. For a geometry unit, a cooking utensil could represent a 45-degree angle. Consider your students' environments when making your lists. Urban settings boast a wealth of objects unique to cities; use this to your advantage.

For a virtual scavenger hunt, create a list of items to be found in reading material associated with the class. For example, in English class, you could ask students to find as many magic tools as possible in a Harry Potter book. Establish a time limit and see which group can find the most items before time runs out. If you have Internet access in your classroom, consider broadening the search field by including online sources.

Create imaginary family trees. Here's a new twist on a common classroom activity. Have students develop an imaginary family tree. It can include historical or literary figures, animals studied in biology, or any figure relevant to your content area. To ensure relevance, you can stipulate specific requirements—for example, one animal, one fictional character, two real relatives, one American Revolutionary War hero, and one current celebrity. The goal is for students to find unique and creative ways to connect themselves with the target figures. In math or science classes, you can build the trees using various geometric designs as their base.

Care for classroom animals. Students with depression, ADHD, or learning disorders all benefit from interacting with animals. The act of petting small, furry animals such as rabbits, gerbils, hamsters, and other common classroom pets for at least 20 minutes releases serotonin in the brain, resulting in a soothing effect ("Interacting with and Petting Animals," 2004).

Animals also provide comfort for shy students or those with few friends. By connecting with animals, these students often learn how to relate to their peers. Similarly, when tasked with caring for animals, overly aggressive children often begin to treat their fellow students with more compassion. Paws for Tales, a program for readers who have not yet mastered basic reading skills or who are simply too embarrassed or shy to read out loud, pairs students with service dogs that have been trained to listen to these readers. The canine "tutors" provide students with a nonjudgmental companion they can feel comfortable practicing with until they are ready to read in front of the class.

Urban youth in particular benefit from interacting with animals, if only because they seldom get the opportunity to do so. Their living arrangements frequently are not conducive to having pets of their own. Thus, being able to interact with and take responsibility for animals in the classroom provides a positive interaction they might otherwise never get.

I remember working in an elementary school in Texas that had a pet pig named Precious. When a student was having a difficult time focusing in class, Precious was called in and played with that child until he calmed down and was ready to learn. Then she was off to help another troubled child.

Spend time with elders. Some of my proudest and most personally meaningful experiences have come from working with American Indian schools, Navajo, Apache, and Lakota (formerly Sioux) among them. One of the great lessons we can learn from native peoples is the high regard they hold for their elders. Tribal elders are afforded great respect and honor, an approach much different from what we are accustomed to in mainstream U.S. society.

Elders relate to children differently than their younger adult counterparts do, in much the same way that grandparents and parents relate differently to children. They are more patient, less concerned about behavior, and more willing to listen. They are far less judgmental. Perhaps most significant, elders transmit long-standing positive values and reaffirm culture and continuity. They provide proof that living is worthwhile; they offer hope.

When troubled youth are paired with senior citizens in school or on trips to assisted-living facilities, it is easy to see how quickly they bond. This connection can be amplified by arranging for senior citizens from the community to come to school on a regular basis. Every class can have an unofficial grandparent or two. They can eat lunch with students, act as chaperones on field trips, spend time with children on the playground, and tutor struggling students. Of course, in order to implement such a program, logistical issues must be overcome—travel, insurance, and, in some states, taking fingerprints for the school's files. But these are minor drawbacks compared with the powerful benefits that come from facilitating such interactions.

Write letters. Hillary Dames, a professional development specialist from Oregon, writes,

> I have had two different classes write letters of advice. This has been great! It is both extremely insightful and has opened up class conversations to a new, heightened level of transparency. One class watched part of [the movie] *The Breakfast Club* and identified a character that they either felt they understood or one that they thought they could help. They wrote a letter of advice to that character on how to be more successful—academically, socially, and emotionally. I had another class listen to the performance poem "Knock, Knock" by Daniel Beaty. They then wrote advice letters to themselves, based on the poem's structure. This also went over very well; powerful conversations ensued.

Another activity is to have students write and send actual letters to real people. If you have ever written a letter to the editor of your local paper, you no doubt checked and double-checked your spelling, punctuation, and word choice because you knew that others would read your writing. The same holds true for students. They can write letters to businesses, politicians, the principal, relatives, other students, or the editor of a paper. If they get a return letter or if their letter gets published, it can be posted on a special section of the classroom wall.

Put on public performances. Many of the activities we've discussed in this chapter—advertisements, songs, stories created during the time machine activity—can be enhanced by having students perform or present them before others. This can be done on a small scale in front of the class or on a larger scale in front of the entire school or community. Knowing that people will be watching them heightens students' need to do well and, for those activities that require group interaction, encourages all members of the group to participate. Further, knowing that people enjoyed and appreciated the performance far exceeds traditional rewards when it comes to building students' pride and confidence.

Finding the Sweet Spot

If we keep in mind that motivation is more related to *how* we teach than to *what* we teach, then the suggestions in this chapter can make any content fun, challenging, and engaging. But these are just the beginning. Once you start to think in new ways, your mind will adapt to find even newer, more exciting lessons on your own. In baseball, hitting the ball right where you want to is called "finding the sweet spot." Transforming an ordinary lesson into an extraordinary one is clearly finding the sweet spot.

8

Energizing Ourselves

The myriad problems urban schools face can make those of us who teach in these environments feel as though we are endlessly swimming upstream. We often feel drained, as if our energy is being pulled right out of us. Yet without this energy, our ability to teach successfully is highly diminished.

Think of your favorite ballplayer, singer, or actor. Athletes and performers who have a real passion for their craft never just go through the motions. They run out ground balls at every game, sing their hearts out at every performance, and pour themselves into every role they play. I once sat next to Dustin Hoffman on a flight to New Orleans while he carefully examined every word of the script to the movie *Runaway Jury* to make sure each was perfect. His dedication was palpable. Bruce Springsteen was once asked how he could perform with such energy so many nights in a row. He responded, "It might be my third or fourth night in a row, but for the people in the audience, it might be their only time." We must bring a similar dedication and energy to our classrooms every day. We may be teaching a concept for the twentieth time, but for our students it is almost always the first time.

If you ask your students to identify characteristics of their favorite and least favorite teachers (see Chapter 7), their answers will likely indicate that the best teachers share a passion for teaching and a genuine love for the subject they teach. Conversely, the ineffective teachers almost certainly exhibited little excitement or passion. To them, teaching was just a job. In Chapter 5, we talked about institutional cynicism. Now let's discuss personal cynicism. Take a look at the following five symptoms of personal cynicism. Do any sound familiar? If so, it is time to take action.

- You start counting the hours left in the school day before you've even set foot in the classroom.
- You feel as though nothing you do in the classroom works. You've given up on trying new things.
- It is more important for you to "get through" the material than it is for your students to learn it.
- You have lost your own love of learning—about content, about teaching, and about life.
- You often wonder why no one is doing anything to make things better, but you don't do anything to make things better yourself.

What action can we take when we fall victim to these symptoms? Teachers in urban settings have found the following seven suggestions effective at combating personal cynicism.

Remember why you became an educator. Remember why you stay an educator. When you decided to become an educator, you probably didn't do it to get rich, receive accolades, or wield great power over school and district functions. We work to make a living, but we teach to change the lives of children. It is hard to remember this, however, when confronted with the host of daily demands that are unrelated to this essential goal—the difficult parent who wants to meet after school, the union fees that are due by the end of the week, the upcoming faculty meeting, and that day's lunchroom duty. With so much on our plates, our most important task, staying energized and excited about teaching, can start to feel like just one more obligation to meet.

I, too, struggle against this phenomenon. I recall a day when I had no energy to teach. I had been on the road doing seminars for 10 days straight. On the last day of the trip, I woke up exhausted in Indianapolis. Even before I showered and dressed, I was counting the hours until I could get on the plane to go home. All teachers have at least one day when they don't care about anything except getting through the day and going home. I wanted a day like that, too.

I was setting up in the seminar room when a woman approached and asked if she could speak to me. Even as I said yes, my mind was still full of thoughts of going home. The woman said, "I just wanted to tell you that my daughter heard you speak last year and said you were wonderful. My school only gives us one inservice day in our whole career, and I decided to come and hear you. I had to get up at 2 a.m. to get here on time, but I know it will be worth it. Thank you."

Needless to say, her words hit me over the head as surely as if they'd been a baseball bat. I told her that she had given me a great gift and I wanted to take her to lunch to thank her. At lunch, I told her how I had felt before she approached me that morning and how her words had energized me. She then proceeded to hit me upside the head a second time.

"Dr. Curwin," she said, "I hate to be rude, but you still don't get it. You didn't come here for me, and this seminar isn't for my benefit. It's for my students. Your job is not merely to help me, but to help all the students that the teachers here today must face tomorrow. All teachers, no matter what level, are doing it for children."

She was right. Since that day, I never forget that we do what we do for the sake of children. Saying this to myself, every time I teach anyone, is the most powerful way I stay energized.

Adopt a hopeless student. In Chapter 6, we looked at the altruism consequence—the idea that emotional healing results when troubled students help other students. This same principle can work for us when it comes to cynicism. It is difficult to remain cynical when we see that our efforts are helping to make a child's life better. One way to do this is to informally adopt a student who seems hopeless or demonstrates no motivation to learn.

Try to casually meet with your adoptee every day for a few minutes to check in, offer encouragement and advice, share in successes, and, hopefully, inspire. If the student gets in trouble, advocate for him. If he needs special services, work with him to get them. Speak to other teachers on his behalf. In other words, act as a big brother or sister. Imagine how different your school would be if 30 of the least involved students had this kind of advocate in their corner.

Adopt a cynical teacher. Another way to fight your own cynicism is to combat it in others. Find a teacher in your school who has given up on children, one who appears to be merely going through the motions. Share with him your success stories and ask to hear hers. Ask her for advice. Offer to work on a joint project or write a piece about your school for the local newspaper together. Nominate her to be in charge of a committee. Believe in her the way you would an unmotivated student, and see if you can reignite the optimism she had when she entered the teaching profession.

Do one activity you love every day. Plan to use at least one activity, demonstration, or strategy that you love every day. When you walk into your classroom, focus on how much you are looking forward to the activity. Your energy and excitement will spill over onto your students. For those students who do not experience enough joy in their lives, your sincerity and enthusiasm can be a real salve.

Stop doing things you hate. If you hate doing an activity or teaching a particular segment of content, then your teaching on that topic will almost certainly lack effectiveness. Even worse, you might unwittingly teach your students to hate it, too. What good is it, for example, to teach kids to read if in the process they learn to hate reading? Try these suggestions to remedy the situation:

- *Cut out a segment of instruction.* Few teachers are able to cover every topic in depth; there's usually something that must be cut or rushed to the point of uselessness. If you have to cut something, why not do it with something you don't like teaching anyway? Cutting out the things you hate will give you more time to go into detail on the equally important topics that you enjoy teaching.

- *Do it in a new way.* If you cannot change what you teach, change how you teach it. Find a new approach that is fun for you and your students. Use the 22 activities listed in the previous chapter as a starting point.

- *Borrow another teacher's love of the content.* Find a teacher in your school who enjoys teaching the content you hate. Find out what it is that this other teacher loves and use it to change your attitude. If you hate teaching commas, for example, find another language arts teacher who loves teaching them and pick her brain for lesson ideas. Maybe she'll give you the wonderful book *Eats, Shoots & Leaves* by Lynne Truss (2006), which demonstrates both the proper and the improper use of commas to hilarious effect:

  – "Eat here, and get gas." *versus* "Eat here and get gas."
  – "Slow, children crossing." *versus* "Slow children crossing."
  – "Becky walked on, her head a little higher than usual." *versus* "Becky walked on her head, a little higher than usual."

Communicate with the people who affect you in school. A constellation of people affects our daily lives, from administrators and secretaries to teachers and custodians. Often, we talk *about* these individuals rather than *to* them. If your comments are positive, keeping them to yourself robs someone else of positive reinforcement and a chance to feel appreciated. If the comments are negative, then complaining, blaming, or whining will not help. Simply state how the situation is hurting you and ask for help in improving things. Here are two examples of how to bring up a problem with a colleague:

- "Why do you always dismiss your class so late? I have to start my class on time. Be more considerate of others."
- "My class starts right after yours, and I've noticed that the students coming from your class tend to get to my class late. I need to start my class on time. Do you have any ideas about how we can solve this problem?"

Which of these approaches would you respond more positively to?

Feel good about what you can control. Make a list of the five things you need for job satisfaction. Do not look ahead until you have completed this step.

Now, identify which of these items you can control and which you cannot. For example, the following are things you cannot control:

- Higher pay.
- More supplies.
- More appreciation from the administration, community, or parents.
- Less pressure to teach to the test.
- Parents who read to their children at home.

One of the most significant sources of personal cynicism is a dependence on things outside our control for satisfaction. Inevitably, wishing for these things leads to a feeling of helplessness and dependency. You can greatly decrease these feelings by focusing on things within your sphere of influence. As my friend and colleague Al Mendler says, "It feels great to stop banging your head against a wall." The following are areas over which you have some control:

- Preparation for class.
- Cooperation with other teachers.
- Dynamic lesson plans.
- Improved relations with difficult parents.

Figuring out and coming to terms with what is and is not within your control is a great lesson to pass on to your students. Their lives are full of forces beyond their ability to control, which leads many of them to try to influence any situation they can. Sometimes this need for control manifests itself in negative ways. For them, negative influence is better than no influence. Your students will develop better attitudes toward your class and learning in general when they feel empowered instead of like victims of circumstance.

Four Keys to Measuring Our Success

One of the best ways to sustain our energy as educators is to acknowledge and celebrate our successes. Unfortunately, because the results of our efforts sometimes take years to come to fruition, this can be a difficult task. Further, much as mortality rates cannot be used to judge the effectiveness of an emergency room doctor versus a knee surgeon, test results alone cannot adequately measure the success of a teacher in an urban environment versus his suburban or rural counterparts. There are simply too many factors affecting student outcomes in urban environments that are beyond the control of the teacher.

This is not to say, however, that we cannot significantly improve our students' chances for success, despite what they may face outside the classroom. And fortunately, students themselves have told us what they need to succeed. Students do not care how well we incorporate rubrics, standards, and curriculum alignment into our classes. Can you imagine two students trying to decide which teacher's class to take based on such criteria?

> Student #1: Take Mr. Chin, he has the best rubrics.
> Student #2: No, I prefer Mrs. Cohen. Her curriculum is properly aligned.

Instead, the elements identified by students as key to their success rely on personal connection, both to the teacher and to the content. They come from students who were asked, "What makes you want to learn from a teacher?"

1. A positive relationship with the teacher. An ongoing, positive relationship with their teacher can motivate and energize students. To build such relationships with your students,

- Be accessible.
- Know your students' names and use them in and out of the classroom.
- Care about how your students are feeling as well as how they are doing academically.
- Listen as much as or more than you talk when having a conversation with a student.
- If you need to postpone a discussion with a student, provide a valid reason for doing so, and be sure to follow up within a reasonable time frame.

Assess your current interactions with your students. How often do you fulfill these key elements of a strong teacher-student relationship?

2. The ability to succeed. Students say they are more motivated when they believe success is possible. To that end, you can offer encouragement, support, extra problem-solving time, "do over" opportunities, and feedback to meet individual needs. Make sure your students believe that if they try, they can succeed.

3. The content's relevance to what is important to them. Successful teachers find ways to connect course content with their students' lives. A great math teacher, for example, makes students say, "I never knew that math was such an important part of my life." Ask yourself if you connect what you teach to real, immediate, and important facets of your students' lives.

4. The teacher's passion for teaching and for the material. The most important success factor for most students is having teachers who show passion and energy for both what and whom they teach. They are creative, expressive, and engaging each and every day. Ask yourself if your love of teaching and of what you teach is obvious to your students.

Make Every Class Interesting

One of the most influential educators in my life, Dwight Allen, was at one time professor emeritus at Old Dominion University in Norfolk, Virginia. When he first started at ODU, he told the university president that he would take the most disliked course on campus and turn it into the most desirable course to prove the point that it is not the course but the way it is taught that determines its motivational value.

After polling faculty and students, he chose freshman composition. Students eventually lined up to take the class. He taught the entire course using just one book: *Anno's Journey* (Anno, 1977), a Japanese children's picture book about the history of Europe. So how did Allen turn a hated writing course into the most popular class on campus using a book with no words? He asked engaging and relevant questions about the book's content:

- Can a book with no words have puns?
- Can it be sexist or racist?
- Can it have metaphors?
- What are words, and how do they work?

Allen's experiment proves that we can reach students regardless of what we teach. The key is in *how* we teach.

Why Do I Have to Learn This?

Most teachers hear this question several times a day. Our answers can clue us in to how we may be sapping our own energy and may provide a path to increased student and self-motivation. Usually, our answers are goal-oriented and future-centered:

- "Because it will help you in the future."
- "You need it for the test."
- "It will make you a better reader."
- "So you can pay your bills."
- "It will be necessary for college."
- "It will help you get a job."
- "It will help you make money."

All of these may be true and may accurately reflect your reasons for teaching the topic in question, but they are not the best answers. For better or worse, children don't live in the future. They live in the present. The future for high school students lies maybe a week out. For middle school students, it's the end of the day. In elementary school, it's within the hour, and in kindergarten, 10 seconds.

A better answer to the question "Why do I have to learn this?" is one that focuses on the present, is less goal-oriented, and is more energy-centered. Enthusiasm is key when delivering these answers:

- "Because I love it and so will you."
- "Because it is fabulous."
- "Because it will prove that learning can be fun."
- "Because we will be doing it for three more days and great days are better than bad ones."

These answers are more inspirational to students and to us as well. If we really believe that we love a subject and so will they—and we should if we're saying it—we cannot help but feel motivated and energized ourselves.

Energy Pays Off

Keep in mind when implementing these suggested activities that you may never see direct evidence of their positive effect on students. As I've already noted, much of what we do as teachers comes to fruition years after our students leave the classroom. But have you ever taught a major troublemaker—one who made you want to quit teaching and head for some far-flung beach resort—only to have that same student return years later to tell you that you were her favorite teacher? Look to that student, and others like her, for evidence of your effectiveness and a reminder of your obligation as an educator.

Obviously, no one can feel upbeat all the time. We are subject to the natural flow of feelings and moods. Life happens, and we are inescapably affected by it. When we become teachers, however, we must accept the responsibility of providing students with a hope-filled place in which to learn, one that is free of negativity and cynicism.

9

Effort-Based Evaluation

The logistics of developing an evaluation plan that meets the varied needs of urban school populations are very nearly overwhelming. Because most formal evaluation procedures, including government-mandated standards, are achievement-based, they fail to meet the individual needs of each student and are not motivational. As Leonard Mlodinow says in his critical analysis of statistical relevance (2008), "It is more reliable to judge people by analyzing their abilities than by glancing at the scoreboard. Or as Bernoulli puts it, 'One should not appraise human action on the basis of results.'" Challenge is uniform regardless of ability, and flexibility is rare. Although we cannot immediately overthrow this entrenched and largely ineffective system, we can find ways to modify it and include evaluation methods that focus on effort.

Charlie's Story

While observing a student teacher in one of San Francisco's "worst" neighborhoods, Hunters Point, I noticed a 9th grader in a remedial reading class. From a distance he seemed charismatic and charming, but close up, his eyes had a vacant look. Curious about his story, I asked the student teacher about him.

He said, "Oh, Charlie. He has such a horrible home life. Two years ago, he was a witness to his mother's murder, and now he's testifying at her killer's trial. His father has been in prison for 10 years. His older brother, who runs a crack house, is raising him and makes Charlie work as a guard all night. Sometimes he makes Charlie smoke crack to keep him awake. He comes to school every day, but he doesn't do anything but sit here."

The following week, we had a conversation about how to grade Charlie:

> Student teacher: Can you help me? I don't know how to grade Charlie. What would you give him?
>
> Me: I'd give him an *A*.
>
> ST: But he didn't do anything.
>
> Me: Yes, he did. He came to school every day under the most difficult circumstances. That's doing a lot.
>
> ST: What about all of the other kids who did more? Is it fair to them?
>
> Me: You can give them *As* too. You don't have a limit, do you?
>
> ST: What will next year's teachers think? Won't they be confused?
>
> Me: Teachers don't care what kids got last year. Most give students a fresh start every year.

I returned a week later to find the class working on a writing assignment. Charlie was vigorously writing, taking breaks to chew his pencil while deep in thought. When the time allotted for the assignment was up and my student teacher asked for the papers, Charlie screamed, "I need five more minutes. Please, just five more minutes." After class, I asked my student teacher what had happened with Charlie. "I couldn't give him an *A*," he said. "It felt wrong. So I gave him a *B+*. He's been writing ever since." I read Charlie's paper and, not surprisingly, it was terrible. But that's not the point. You can't learn to write well until you write something. Charlie had taken a first step toward improvement.

I do not advocate this approach for most students, but grades are more than simple, summary evaluations. They are a significant part of the learning and motivation process. Providing Charlie with hope and the possibility of success was far more important than adhering to a traditional mode of evaluation.

Eight Trouble Spots

The current mode of evaluation poses eight threats to motivation: (1) false objectivity, (2) inappropriate standards, (3) underutilization of a diagnostic approach, (4) measurement reduction, (5) coverage of too much material, (6) underemphasis on personal meaning, (7) overemphasis on achievement, and (8) the use of testing as a form of accountability.

False Objectivity

Objectively correct answers to questions do exist. "Gravity" is the objectively correct answer to the question "What makes an apple fall from a tree?" The problem lies in measuring the worth or importance of that answer. A teacher can decide objectively if the answer is correct, but determining its worth or the student's comprehension of the answer moves into the realm of subjectivity.

When I was in high school, I loved the play *Oedipus Rex,* a Greek tragedy full of complex plot twists, intrigue, and passion. I was thrilled to discover that my first test in college would be on *Oedipus.* I knew I was going to get an *A.* After all, I'd studied it in depth—its symbolism, history, staging, and dialogue. I knew it inside and out.

Imagine my dismay when I got the test and read the first question: "What was the name of the mountain Oedipus was chained to as a baby?" I answered, "Who cares? What a stupid question." The rest of the questions were equally insipid, having no relevance to the meaning or value of this great work of art. Needless to say, I failed my first college test . . . and on a topic I knew and loved. I went to the teacher and raised my objections. She said it was an objective test and I got the answers wrong. I replied, "If this was an objective test, why did you get to pick the questions?"

There is no such thing as an objective test or grade. Performance measures can only be guessed at. What qualifies as an *A* according to one teacher may be an *F* according to another. Even with a subject that seems unassailably objective when it comes to evaluation, subjectivity can play a significant role. Evaluating spelling, for example, seems like a solidly objective endeavor. Answers are right or wrong. Going on this assumption, let's say that a student spelled 50 out of

100 words correctly but later demonstrated that 4 of the words that had been marked incorrect were really correct. Every teacher I asked said they would give the student the 4 points. But what would happen if a second student correctly demonstrated that 4 other words that had been marked correct were actually wrong? Would you deduct 4 points? I posed this question to hundreds of teachers, and the results were split in half. Thus, the exact same spelling test can end up receiving two different scores based entirely on the values of the teacher. Even the decision of which words to include on the test is subjective in that it is based on which words the teacher decides are of value (Harmon, 1974).

The consequences of subjectivity can be severe. Let's say two students in different classes get the same answer wrong on a math test—not because they didn't understand the process required to solve the problem but rather because of a careless error. One student receives 7 points out of 10, while the other receives 8 points out of 10. If we extrapolate this discrepancy throughout the students' careers, one student will end up with a 70 percent average and the other with an 80 percent average. This discrepancy could lead to different expectations on the part of students and teachers alike, which will in turn affect the students' level of motivation. Ultimately, this discrepancy could lead the two students down significantly different life paths.

The following are examples of how different measures of validity can radically affect a student's scores:

1. True or false? The sun rises in the east and sets in the west. *Student answer:* "Neither. The sun doesn't rise at all. The Earth rotates around the sun." Answer marked wrong.

2. To go from New York City to Moscow, do you travel: (A) North, (B) South, (C) East, or (D) West? *Student answer:* "C and D, but D takes longer." Answer marked wrong.

3. How many planets are there in our solar system? *Student answer:* "Nine." Answer marked wrong because Pluto no longer qualifies as an official planet according to the latest definition.

4. Who has a stronger vocabulary? One child hears a word frequently at home; another child hears a different word that means the same thing. On a vocabulary test, the word used in the first child's home appears. The first

child answers the question correctly. The second child, even though she knows another word that means exactly the same thing, gets the answer wrong.

Tests, by design, are snapshots of someone's idea of what is important to know, what constitutes a correct answer, and how much that answer is worth. It is more productive to accept these limitations and acknowledge the high degree of subjectivity involved in the measurement of learning than it is to pretend that we can really parse the difference between a 68 percent and a 75 percent.

Inappropriate Standards

The need for standards is not in question. Standards are important evaluation tools. Students need them to measure their improvement and capabilities, and schools need them to certify a minimum level of competence and to determine advancement in a particular area. The public demands standards as a form of proof that schools are doing their job educating our youth. The question is not whether we should use standards, but rather how we should use them. Is the current system of a unified, single set of standards for all students adequate, or should standards be individualized?

Those who advocate for a single, unified set of standards argue that if standards vary, they are no longer standards but merely targets, something to generally aim for. I strongly disagree. Outside school, standards vary all the time. Compare job descriptions. Every job has different skill requirements or performance standards. Graphic designers, firefighters, and restaurant managers all have to meet individualized performance standards. A landscaper is not expected to have, nor is she evaluated on, the same skill set as a chef. Here are some other situations that call into question the necessity of blanket standards for all:

- Should students with special needs be required to meet the same standards as regular education students?
- Should all students with special needs be required to meet the same standards, regardless of their disabilities or needs?
- Should students on a college track be required to meet the same standards as those who will not go to college?

- Should students who emigrated from other countries be required to meet the same language standards as native speakers?
- If standards are set too high for many students, is it fair to fail them if they try their best?
- If standards are low enough that everyone who tries can meet them, are they fair to those who excel?
- Should students in large inner-city schools with limited resources be required to meet the same standards as students in smaller, suburban schools with far more resources?
- Should inner-city students be passed on with lower standards when they have the ability to do much better? Many argue that because of inner-city students' backgrounds and socioeconomic status, they cannot do as well as their suburban counterparts. Yet many urban students can and do excel when expectations are higher. Should we sell them short because of assumptions about what they are capable of?

One last scenario: a student in your reading class has done nothing for most of the year, whereas other students have read 20 or more books. What should be your goal for the unmotivated student? To get her to read the 20 books required to pass the class or to read even one book? One thing is certain. If the student has no hope of passing, she will continue to do nothing. If the established standard cannot be reached, do we pass this student for making incremental progress? If we do, the standard has no meaning. If we do not, we lose the student. Given the way schools are currently structured, there is no clear answer, no easy solution; both answers on their face are unacceptable. Individualization of standards, however, could provide the solution to this untenable situation. We currently provide students with IEPs, so why not individualized standards?

Underutilization of a Diagnostic Approach

Let's revisit a scenario we looked at earlier. While working a complex math problem, a student makes a simple calculation error. It is clear from the rest of the student's calculations that she understands the process behind the problem. It is impossible, even with a rubric, to score the student's answer objectively because the rubric itself is a subjective construct. It may seem to "objectively" lay out the value of comprehension versus a correct answer, but someone had to subjectively make that determination in the first place. As a diagnostic, however, it is extremely useful. It tells the teacher where to focus additional instruction.

I believe that every test or quiz used in the instructional process should be used diagnostically; that is, it should be used to improve the performance of the students. Grading and recording scores do not help students learn. In fact, they contribute to the demotivation of many students. The focus of evaluation needs to shift from scoring to improvement of learning.

Measurement Reduction

When we attempt to measure academic knowledge, we tend to measure the lowest level of understanding and, often, the least important information. My experience being tested on *Oedipus Rex* in college is a good example. It was easy to measure whether I knew the name of the mountain the protagonist was chained to as an infant. It would have been far more difficult to measure how well I understood the concepts of fatalism and free will and how they play out as the drama unfolds. The former only proved that I had read the text; it did nothing to evaluate whether I'd understood what I'd read. Likewise, it is difficult to measure whether a student understands a mathematical process. It is easy to measure a numerical answer.

The principle of measurement reduction has the tail wagging the dog. Knowing we have to come up with a justifiable score on which to base a grade, we tend to reduce the level of learning to that which can be easily measured in a seemingly objective manner. Thus, the mundane and boring replace the significant and enlightening in lesson design, and motivation is severely hampered in the process.

Effective teachers guard against measurement reduction by including complex concepts in their curriculum. But in the face of curriculum alignment and high-stakes testing, this is becoming much harder to do. And even teachers who truly elevate learning for their students have trouble translating that learning into a grade.

Measuring and grading students' creativity illustrates the problem of reduction. If a student writes something that is highly creative but riddled with grammatical errors, the more points he loses for the grammar, the less his creativity is being valued. It is certainly not wrong to want students to use correct grammar, but in overly valuing the grammar, we risk minimizing creative thought. Even if there are no grammatical errors, how do we assess a creative thought on paper? Here are two responses from 2nd graders in Rochester, New York, that I believe are highly creative. How would you grade them?

- When asked to describe a favorite food, Andy said, "Cooked carrots taste like people walking slow."
- When asked to describe a winter scene, Bitzy replied, "It's pitch white."

Coverage of Too Much Material

Many teachers mistakenly believe that they must cover an enormous amount of material to ensure that their students receive high scores on standardized tests. The truth, however, is that deeper coverage of less material better serves students on standardized tests. This is especially true in the case of tests that are timed or that subtract points for wrong answers but not for skipped items. If a student is familiar with a question because it was covered in class but does not know the correct answer, he will stop and try to figure it out; he may make a guess. He has a slight chance of being correct. But if he knows nothing about the question, he will most likely skip it and go on to another question. More correct answers come from knowing material that was fully taught in class than from vaguely recalling a teacher's cursory overview of multiple topics.

Underemphasis on Personal Meaning

Personal meaning is what students take from a lesson that is personally relevant or important to them. For example, if you are driving to work and hear about a car accident on the radio in which someone named Sheila Brown was critically injured, you might react by thinking, "That's too bad. People should be more careful," or "I'd better slow down." But if Sheila Brown is a relative or close friend, your reaction is obviously going to be much more visceral. The information is the same in both cases, but its personal meaning is very different.

Personal meaning cannot be measured by testing. If a racist student studies *To Kill a Mockingbird* and gets an *A* on a test about the book but remains racist, it is unlikely that anything in the book had personal meaning for him. Conversely, if the student's parents are racist but he is not, and he sees something of them in the forces against which Atticus Finch is fighting, that constitutes personal meaning. Nonetheless, he may do poorly on a test about the book.

Personal meaning is undervalued in the evaluation process, but it is the defining variable when it comes to changing behavior. Individualized evaluation practices can address this seemingly unsolvable problem. Just asking something like "Can you give an example of something you have done as a result of reading this book?" can make a difference. If learning does not connect to students on a personal level, then it is merely a series of time-filling activities that have no hope of bringing about changes in behavior. For learning to change behavior, it must make a personal connection to the student and be accounted for in the evaluation process.

Overemphasis on Achievement

Achievement is often set as a "false" goal in academics. It is false because no one can really control achievement. A student cannot control the score she receives on a test; she can only control the amount of effort she expends. Hence, the real goal should be effort, with achievement being the natural outcome or by-product. Effort creates achievement. The more a student tries, the greater the achievement.

Focusing too much on achievement works against students by stifling motivation. Students cannot give more than their maximum effort, and those who do expend effort only to do poorly begin to stop caring about performing in school. In fact, they may begin actively pursuing an entirely different type of achievement—one that falls on the opposite end of the performance scale. If they can't meet the achievement goals set by the district or school, then perhaps they can be the best at failing to meet them.

Students learn at a very early age that they can always succeed in school by changing the definition of success. If they are bad at being good, they can be good at being bad. If they are bad at taking tests, they can be the best at failing them. If they have trouble doing their work, they have no trouble not doing their work.

I do not foresee effort becoming the standard for academic success. Some argue that it is too hard to measure, not realizing that achievement is just as impossible to measure objectively. Further, most don't understand this simple fact: the more successful we are at getting students to put forth their best effort, the greater their level of achievement will be.

The Use of Testing as a Form of Accountability

The achievement-versus-effort conundrum presents problems for teachers and schools as well. In this case, "achievement" is determined by students' scores on standardized tests. Teachers and schools cannot be accurately evaluated based on student test scores. What students bring to the classroom determines their scores more than our influence. Teacher evaluation must be based on our best efforts—whether or not we did the best we could—not student test results. The degree of pressure placed on schools and teachers to meet testing goals makes it difficult to tailor evaluation to meet the needs of specific students.

The Remedy: A Way to Evaluate That Increases Student Motivation

Let's look at the way preschool-age children learn. When a toddler takes a first step and falls down, we don't give a poor grade for walking; we encourage the child to try again. Similarly, we don't chastise children for poor grammar when they are first learning to talk. The way we teach these youngsters is to encourage effort rather than to measure achievement. Our mantra is "Try again," not "That's not good enough." We operate on the understanding that effort comes before achievement.

When toddlers enter school, they are suddenly greeted with achievement tests. Now their effort is irrelevant; we classify them by test scores. We compare them with others. We create winners and losers. Proponents of this system say that it mirrors the realities of life and is good preparation. Untrue. In life, people choose where to place their effort. We win or lose in arenas of our own choosing. If you find that you are not skilled in the sciences, you are not forced to become a scientist. In school, however, children have no choice. The school decides where they must put their effort. It decides the arenas in which they must compete. The solution is to incorporate both effort and achievement into the evaluation process, to increase the value of effort without diminishing the quality of achievement.

Strategies for Valuing Effort

Begin with what is right. Andrew answers four questions right out of ten on his test. Rather than focusing immediately on the answers he got wrong, acknowledge the answers he got right and use those to further motivate him. Instead of saying, "If you don't start working harder and getting more answers right on your tests, you will fail this class," acknowledge that getting some answers right demonstrates that he is capable of doing the work and can feel confident that, with effort, he can get more correct on the next test. "Look, you got four answers right! That means you can do this work!"

Use wrong answers as a teaching tool rather than as a negative. We often learn more from our mistakes than from our successes. Think of all the errors you made learning to use your computer. Had the computer chastised you every time you made a mistake, you might have quit trying altogether.

Students are far more likely to respond in class, both orally and on written assignments, if mistakes are considered learning opportunities rather than failures. Rank the following three teacher responses to mistakes made in front of the class in terms of their motivational value:

- "Wrong. Can anyone help her?"
- "Think. Now try again."
- "That's a helpful mistake. It gives the class a chance to learn this topic more completely. Thanks."

Do overs. First attempts in life outside of school are often carefully evaluated but rarely looked at as "final." An architect creates multiple drafts of a building plan before any construction begins. Surgeons spend countless lab hours practicing on cadavers before they cut open a live patient. Baseball players go through spring training. In school, however, students rarely get a chance to create true drafts (i.e., work that is evaluated solely in terms of how it can be used to create a better, more complete version). What is called a first draft is frequently graded as a final draft. Do overs allow students to retake tests and quizzes after analyzing the mistakes they made on their previous attempts.

You might say to an unmotivated student, "I know you are probably tired of taking tests, but I'm sure you can do better if we go over your errors, learn from them, and try again. Are you willing to give it another shot? "

Allowing students to "do over" values effort. If students are willing to retake a test, they are demonstrating a willingness to try harder. The downside to do overs is the increased burden on the teacher. Correcting tests and papers more than once and writing different versions of the same test is hard work. Another potential pitfall is that some students, knowing that they will be allowed to try again, may not put forth their full effort on the first try. Limiting do overs to a few unmotivated students may help to keep extra grading to a minimum. Once they adjust to the added work brought on by allowing do overs, most teachers find that the motivational boost it gives students is well worth the additional time and effort. Start slow. Choose one or two tests or papers the first quarter, and see how it goes. If you like the results and can handle the additional work, add more assignments.

Works in progress. Works in progress is a broader variation of do overs; it includes not only tests but also a wider array of assignments, including homework, projects, essays, and book reviews.

Allowing works in progress can be even more time-consuming than do overs. When I taught 7th grade English, three of my students handed me multiple papers to reevaluate the day before grades were due. I quickly learned to set precise limits on how I would implement the works in progress system. As with do overs, it helps to start slow and build up to your most comfortable level. Select one paper, project, or test for a trial. Allow students to redo it until they (and you) are satisfied with the results. Due to time and resource limits as well as personal energy limits, I suggest prioritizing students who need your time the most. Although grading in this way is more time-consuming, students are more likely to get and stay motivated when they know that their progress is valued.

Factor in improvement when determining grades. Considering multiple factors, including improvement, when determining a student's grade makes the imprecise evaluation process a little more balanced. It also increases effort on the part of students because they know that they have multiple opportunities to affect their final grade. If they do poorly in one area, they are not doomed to fail. Some educators believe that the final examination or project is the only one that should count for the final grade. They say that it doesn't matter what the ups and downs are on the way to completion, provided you eventually get there. Although I agree that the final project should have significant value, what happens to a student who does well all term and then blows the final?

I prefer to encourage students to keep trying and, if they seem to understand the concepts you are teaching, to give additional weight to that when grading. Improvement should be encouraged throughout the grading period. It not only signifies high effort but also is a true measure of increased competence. Students try harder when they know that improvement over time will count more than an early failure.

Do not fail a student who tries. Over the years I have come to believe that no student who tries should ever fail. The standards movement directly contradicts this important principle. Educators hear frequent complaints about social promotion and passing kids before they've mastered the skills they need for the next grade from politicians, parents of "other" students, and other teachers who inherit students they perceive as unprepared. Think about this from a motivational perspective. You have a student who does no work. If you keep the possibility of passing available to the student, you might get him to do some work. If he knows he will fail, he will almost certainly do nothing. Which is better, some learning or none at all?

I understand that school politics might make applying this principle difficult. You will have to decide for yourself whether doing so in your classroom is worth the possible political difficulties that might ensue. Teachers who love this principle but do not know how to apply it often ask me, "How do I know the student is trying? How do I measure effort?" My quick answer is, "The same way you measure achievement: guess." My more complete answer is to look for the following:

- A willingness to utilize do overs and works in progress.
- Evidence of helping others.
- Asking for help.
- Improvement from one draft or test to the next.
- Full participation in group activities.

You can also ask students to tell you how they will demonstrate effort and use the criteria they establish. You may have noticed that I did not include classroom participation on this list. I do not consider class participation a good indicator of effort because some students talk a lot and say little, whereas others do not say much but are deeply involved and interested in the content being covered.

Do not give an *A* to a student who shows no evidence of effort. I have a personal aversion to giving the highest grades to students who do not try. It teaches them that effort is unimportant and sets them up for failure when they eventually face the greater challenges of higher education and the workplace. If you choose to implement this principle, however, you must inform students and parents, and you must be clear about how you intend to measure effort. One way to do this fairly is to include students' own criteria for measuring effort as part of their grade.

Some educators disagree with this approach, arguing that it is not the fault of the students if the work is too easy and that it is unfair to penalize them because they are not being adequately challenged. I agree, and therefore I offer a caveat: this type of grading operates on the principle that great teachers need to challenge all students, including those who naturally excel. It is valid only if students are provided with appropriately challenging opportunities.

Dealing with Classroom Competition

Evaluation breeds competition. Formally, we acknowledge achievement with the honor roll, academic societies, award assemblies, and, ultimately, college acceptance. Informally, we acknowledge it by posting performance charts, displaying exemplars of student work, and awarding privileges. There are two arguments for these forms of acknowledgment: (1) They give students something to aspire to, and (2) high performance should be recognized and rewarded. However, two compelling counterarguments exist as well: (1) They only inspire students who would perform at exemplary levels anyway (i.e., they help the students who don't need it), and (2) they kill motivation in the students who never win anything—the students who need motivation the most.

As with other strategies we've looked at thus far, it is not what we do in this case that matters so much as how we do it. Acknowledgment of achievement is not a bad thing, but it must be done correctly. The following seven approaches to formal and informal recognition of achievement all follow the principles of motivation already established in this book.

Focus on effort. Not all students can perform equally, but every student can put forth effort. Honor rolls, class rankings, and all the other forms of recognition need to be effort-based if they are to motivate those who need it the most. I can hear the howls of protest now, telling me that this is unfair and sends the wrong message. But how fair is comparing students who have no say about whom they're being compared with or in what capacity and then telling them that their best efforts are not good enough?

Should Charlie, the troubled student from the beginning of this chapter, have made the honor roll? Or should he have failed the class? A strong case can be made either way. But as long as he doesn't prevent anyone else from making it, is there any real harm in the former? I'm not arguing that this is an easy question to answer. But on an individual student basis, it is a question worth asking.

Make it voluntary. Many educators use sports as a metaphor for academic competition. One aspect of sports competition that often goes unmentioned when such analogies are made, however, is that participation in sports is voluntary. Leaving aside misguided parents who pressure their children into playing sports, children compete athletically because they want to. The voluntary nature of sports allows children to find the best activity and the best level of competition for them. If they're not good at soccer, they might try tennis, swimming, or any number of other sports. Similarly, if a student is not skilled enough to play a varsity sport, she can play intramurals or even just compete on the playground.

In school, students have little or no choice about their competitors or the areas of competition. All students must take the core curriculum starting in 1st grade and going all the way through high school. Sometimes they can choose to take an honors class, sometimes not. When it comes to formal evaluation systems like the honor roll or class ranking, they have very little choice at all.

Fortunately, teachers can do a lot to make competition within the classroom more voluntary, such as letting students choose one of several different ways to show comprehension or having students compete against themselves by choosing challenge sheets to complete. Make a list of the ways in which you use competition in your class currently and develop additional activities from which students can choose.

Keep it private. Stop putting achievement or performance charts on the walls for all to see. They do not inspire motivation in low achievers. Quite the opposite, in fact. They kill the desire to compete. No one needs to see how much worse he is than others on a day-to-day basis. Grades and test results should be kept private. If students want to make them public, that is their choice. We should not make that choice for them.

Make it inclusive. No student should be excluded from opportunities to be recognized and appreciated, regardless of background, behavior, family history, or even grades. School is not just for the high-performing; it is for every student. The more you can include your unmotivated students by finding competitive challenges at an appropriate level for them, the more they will engage in the competition.

Fair is not equal. As previously discussed, doing what is fair for all students does not always mean treating them in an equal manner. This is especially true in academic competition. Further, the varying cultures, languages, backgrounds, and abilities of urban students make treating them identically nonsensical. With this in mind, effort once again emerges as the most logical competitive factor.

Focus on learning, not winning. Undeniably, winning is fun and builds confidence. However, an overemphasis on winning leads to cheating, cutthroat tactics, and arguments over points or scores. The stakes need to be kept low enough to deemphasize winning while still retaining the positive attributes that competition engenders. Learning must trump winning in every academic competition.

Keep corrections manageable. Although having students go back and correct their mistakes can be extremely useful for bringing about individual improvement, keep in mind that students can handle only a certain number of corrections. If there are too many, they usually crumple up the paper and throw it away. My guideline is to require only two corrections per page. You may at first find it difficult not to fix or point out every error. I did initially, but in the long run, I got better results from students and had less work to do myself.

Tell students you will not point out every error they make, just a couple of important ones. Find the two most important errors and offer suggestions as to how the student can improve. Here are some examples of issues to look for:

- Incomplete thought.
- Improper comma usage.
- Careless calculation mistakes.

- Faulty conclusions.
- Lack of evidence.
- Repeated misspelling of the same word.
- Lack of a topic sentence.
- Lack of clear connection between ideas.

Consider having students put their two main corrections on note cards and setting aside class time for them to work on the corrections.

Examples of Effective Grading Systems

Finals at the beginning. Here is one way I solved the dilemma of evaluating students while simultaneously giving them control of their own learning. As a college professor, my goals were to give as much control as was feasible to my students (who were all educators or future educators) and to motivate them to learn in class. I administered the "final" exam to students on the first day of class. The exam had 15 questions, all related to what a teacher must know to effectively teach. Questions included "What is your grading policy?", "What is your plan for motivation?", and "What is your plan for discipline?" I also gave students the opportunity to write a question of their own, pending my approval. The students had all semester to answer the questions and to check with me for proficiency. They could answer any four questions correctly for a *B* or any six for an *A*. Because I was teaching a graduate-level course, the only lower grades possible were failure or an incomplete. Finals were due on the last day of class.

This system gave students a lot of control and choice, in terms of both time management and the actual questions they would answer. The standards were individualized, as were the challenges. Because each question had criteria for successful completion, it had a built-in diagnostic system. It wasn't perfect because, in the end, the final grade was determined by the number of questions answered. But no grading system can be perfect. This system ensured that students met a minimum standard of knowledge to become teachers while protecting their individual needs. All teachers can use aspects of this system, regardless of the grade level or subject they teach.

Menu grading. Menu grading can be used for any grade level and is especially useful for creative and higher-level thinking assignments. It dovetails nicely with rubrics. Make a list of all of the elements included in the instructional process that can be evaluated. Examples include

- Proper use of commas.
- Use of metaphors.
- Correct spelling.
- Logical thought.

Give the list to each student before the test, project, assignment, or experiment commences. Let the students decide the percentage that each item will be worth, based on what is most important to them individually. You can require that every element be given some weight or even require a minimum weight for some items. Thus, you develop one overarching evaluation mechanism, but you are grading each student's project, assignment, or test according to the grading criteria each student came up with.

Challenge grading. Challenge grading is based on the idea that having a choice of challenge increases motivation and thus improves learning. Develop an evaluation device that has multiple levels of challenge, with increasing point values earned as the difficulty increases. Thus, 20 correct answers equal 40 points at a level that has been increased by a factor of two. Students can choose to answer as many questions or problems as they want at whatever challenge levels make sense to them.

Contract grading. With contract grading, students agree to do a predetermined amount of work and are graded on how well they do. Some contracts, however, are more effective than others. Remember that a contract is an agreement between two parties. Students need to have a significant say about what goes into the contract for it to work. Here are five suggestions to make contract grading work:

- Students are allowed to veto a predetermined number of contract items that have been added by the teacher.
- Students are allowed to add an equal number of items to be evaluated by the teacher.
- The contract has built-in milestones to be checked by the teacher.
- The contract incorporates both menu- and challenge-grading techniques.

• Contracts are not written in stone. Allow for revisions throughout the term of the contract. Sometimes students bite off more than they can chew. It is better to take on too much and revise downward than to start with something too easy.

Keeping Hope Afloat

Do not let students ever feel that is "too late" for them to try. Nothing kills hope more than guaranteed failure. As long as students have a chance, they might be willing to try. And learning something is always better than learning nothing.

10

Improving Homework Completion

In the past, students came up with a staggering array of excuses for not doing their homework, some incredibly creative:

- "My turtle ate it."
- "My father took it to work by mistake."
- "My baby sister threw up on it."
- "My mother dropped it in the garbage disposal."
- "My grandmother wrapped my pet fish with it when it died."

Today's students don't bother with excuses. Instead they just say, "I didn't do it. So what?" There are nearly as many reasons why students refuse to do homework as there are excuses for not doing it, among them

- A lack of ideal or even minimally conducive conditions at home.
- Poorly designed homework.
- A disconnect between homework and schoolwork.
- Students who have given up.
- A mismatch between the ability of the students and the challenge of the work.
- Students who are lazy or don't care.

Many educators question the value of homework as a learning tool. Sara Bennett and Nancy Kalish's 2006 book *The Case Against Homework* debunks the myth that giving kids homework improves their educational outcome. In actuality, much of the homework we give children serves no educational purpose. And many urban students' home lives counter their ability to complete their homework and learn from it. Older children often either work to help make ends meet or are tasked with caring for their younger siblings and even older members of the household. Those who live in gang- or drug-infested neighborhoods have too many safety concerns to concentrate on their studies. In addition, some homes are chaotic or overcrowded, offering no quiet place where a student can focus on schoolwork.

Further, lack of homework completion is one of the main triggers of power struggles between teachers and students—a struggle that can suck up class time and drain the energy of both parties. With all this in mind, why give homework at all? The answer is that homework can be an effective tool in the learning process when it takes into account and incorporates a number of key factors.

Homework should offer an appropriate level of challenge. As we discussed in Chapter 9, incorporating appropriate levels of challenge improves the motivational value and likelihood of completion of any assignment, homework included. When it comes to homework, however, we are often reluctant to alter assignments for students whom we perceive as lazy or uncaring. Certainly, it can be difficult to justify to other students or parents why some students are given different levels of challenge than others. Nonetheless, we must make the effort to accommodate students' differing motivation and ability levels. If the work is too easy, the student is unlikely to do it—or learn anything important if he does—but if it is too difficult, he is even less likely to complete it.

In his 2008 book *Outliers*, sociologist Malcolm Gladwell lauds the Knowledge Is Power Program (KIPP) schools for their unparalleled academic results in urban settings. The KIPP schools, founded in 1995 by two former Teach for America corps members, have an impressive track record of student achievement. According to Kipp.org, "while fewer than one in five low-income students attend college nationally, KIPP's college matriculation rate stands at more than 80 percent for students who complete the 8th grade at KIPP. In 2007, nearly 95 percent of KIPP alumni went on to college-preparatory high schools;

collectively, they have earned millions of dollars in scholarships and financial aid since 2000."

Gladwell attributes much of the success of these students to the amount of time they devote to studying, in particular the three weeks in the summer, which gives them an academic edge over many of their urban counterparts. I would argue that an even bigger influence is that KIPP students are challenged at an extraordinarily high level, yet one that is within reach if students are willing to exert high levels of effort. High levels of challenge combined with inclusion of effort as part of the evaluation process breed pride in those students who can meet them, without stigmatizing as failures the students who genuinely cannot. The KIPP schools' results demonstrate that few students lack ability when effort is a major variable for measuring and encouraging learning.

Homework should engender a high level of student interest. Great homework assignments begin with a strong connection to students' hobbies and interests. Music, sports, fashion, television shows, and video games can all provide solid starting points for creating motivating homework assignments. Interest can also be developed with teasers, great questions, and the other motivation techniques described in Chapter 7.

Homework should have appropriate proportionality. Proportionality refers to the amount of homework assigned in relation to the age and ability of your students. Some educators believe that one minute for every year of age per subject is good starting place. That equals 5 minutes per subject area for 1st graders, 12 minutes for 7th graders, and 18 minutes for high school seniors. Of course, some students can handle more, some less, depending on their home lives, physical or learning disabilities, and the amount of homework given in their other classes. One thing is certain—assigning too much homework practically guarantees it will not be finished, no matter how exciting and worthwhile it is.

Homework should relate to class content. Homework cannot exist in a vacuum. It needs to be fully integrated into the ongoing curriculum. The best homework sets the stage for the next day's lesson. For example, if you assign students to read a chapter in a book, the chapter should be an integral part of the following day's lesson. If they do math problems, the skill they practiced needs to be included in the next day's lesson plan. If students perceive a consistent disconnect between classroom work and homework, even motivated students may start to wonder why they should bother to do the latter.

Homework should be quickly corrected and returned to students. The longer the period of time between completion of homework and receipt of feedback, the less useful the homework becomes. Any longer than the next day for typical assignments or a week for major long-term projects creates a gap that diminishes motivation to complete future assignments.

Homework should offer students real choices. Students can be given two choices with regard to homework assignments. You can allow them to choose between one-third and one-half of the total number of questions to answer. This provides students with a feeling of control while also cutting back on correction time. Or you can allow them to choose their homework days. Offer to put it to a vote: "Class, we can have homework on Monday, Tuesday, and Thursday or Monday, Wednesday, and Friday. Let's vote on which days you prefer." Giving students a choice of homework days, once again, increases their sense of control and also maintains proportionality. Both options increase the chance that all students will complete their assignments.

Homework should include minimal use of ditto sheets, worksheets, or other types of busy work. Whether ditto sheets (amazingly, some schools do still use them), worksheets, or computer tasks, any assignment that students perceive as busy work has a negative effect over time on their willingness to do homework. Occasional use of worksheets may result in positive outcomes, but the more they are used in lieu of genuinely engaging, relevant assignments, the more students will begin to trivialize homework.

Homework should showcase multiple skills and intelligences. Ask students to produce projects that use different skills or aptitudes. Incorporate drawings, music, and drama or even carpentry, sewing, and cooking to allow those with aptitudes in different areas to shine.

Homework should allow for works in progress. Longer assignments can become a "work in progress." Ask students to hand in what they have completed for feedback and implement progress checks on a regular basis leading up to the due date. This helps keep students from procrastinating beyond the point of recovery.

Homework should include clear directions. Students often complain that they didn't understand how to do their homework once they got home. Granted, this is sometimes because they didn't listen when the directions were given, but sometimes directions that are clear to us make little sense to them. It is best to go through the steps yourself to check for any possible points of confusion. Time permitting, consider letting another teacher take a look at the directions as well. Make sure also to provide the directions in writing to the students, and always include a sample question or problem for them to use as an example.

Homework should include parental involvement but should not require it. The more parents or other caregivers in the home are involved in the homework process, the greater the likelihood it will get done. At a minimum, ask for a signature indicating that a parent read over the assignment. Greater involvement might include a few questions that the child can ask the parent as part of the assignment or vice versa. Here are some examples:

- *English:* Ask your child what he or she thinks of this book. Write down three words that summarize his or her response.
- *Math:* Did you learn how to do this kind of problem when you were in school?
- *Social studies:* What do you remember learning about this issue when you were your child's age?
- *Science:* Ask your child what he or she is learning to do. Do you use this concept in your life, and if so, how?
- *Music:* What is your favorite song? Why is it your favorite?
- *Art:* Can you draw a version of what your child is drawing? Yours will not be judged! Just do it for fun.

You may need to adjust the language level or translate the questions for non-English-speaking parents. Keep in mind that the experience should be enjoyable for the parent, not embarrassing or uncomfortable.

Also keep in mind that no child should ever be penalized for what his or her parents will or will not do. If parents do not want to be involved, let it go. Never put a child in the position of choosing between home and school. No one wins, and the child loses.

Homework should utilize guessing. As I suggested in Chapter 7, students enjoy guessing and don't perceive it as work. Once students guess, they tend to want to know if they are right. This provides a chance to learn. Ask for hypotheses, estimations, inferences, and deductions. Tell students that the homework requires no actual work; they just have to guess.

Homework should encourage creativity. Encourage students to think outside the box. Pose questions that require creative thinking to answer. One of my favorite creativity activities is to ask students to connect seemingly unrelated concepts—for example, "What do fractions have to do with a walk in the park on a sunny day?" or "How do you think Shakespeare would feel about ice cream cones? Answer in his words."

Homework should allow for work in teams. Organize homework assignments in teams based on interest, ability, or friendships. Students work best when they choose their own teammates, but feel free to use your influence to achieve social goals. For example, make sure that less popular students are included and that their teams accept them. Hold all students accountable for the work of the team by giving two assessments, one for the team and one for the individual effort of each student.

Homework should get personal without invading privacy. Create assignments that delve into students' likes and dislikes, what their family does for fun, family history, or holiday traditions. Students might ask their grandparents questions about specific events or life in general in an earlier time, for example, "Grandma, we are studying the Cold War in history class. Can you tell me what it was like to live in the United States during that time?"

Late homework should be evaluated based on what you value. Homework handed in late presents a quandary for most teachers. Should you accept it? Should you take off a set number of points for every day it is late? What if it represents a rare completion by a highly unmotivated student whom you don't wish to discourage?

When he was in 11th grade, my son had a long-term architecture assignment that involved drawing many different San Francisco structures. He waited far too long to get started and ended up doing a sloppy job to finish on time. His teacher's late-assignment policy was to take one letter grade off for every day the assignment was late. Before he handed the project in, he came to me and said, "Dad, this is really poorly done. I can do a much better job, but I'll lose points if I turn it in late. What should I do?" I told him the answer could be found in his values. "What do you value more, handing in junk on time or something to be proud of that is late?" He proceeded to design one of the best set of drawings imaginable, easily graduate-level work, and turned it in—three days late.

I was teaching a course at San Francisco State University at the time, and my son's architecture teacher was taking a course in the room next door. We met by chance after class and she greeted me with consternation. "I don't know what to do with your son's project," she said. "It is too good to give a *C* or *D* to, but it's late. What do you recommend?" I gave her the same basic answer that I gave my son. "It depends on your values. If you value being on time more than quality then give him a *C* or *D*, otherwise give him an *A*. I have no preference. It's up to you." Ultimately, she gave the assignment a *B*.

Obviously, timeliness and quality are both important values for most of us, as is following through on our stated policies. Applying the "fair is not equal" principle is appropriate in such situations. Also consider adding an addendum to your lateness policy: "If you are going to turn in an assignment late and you explain to me why in writing, I will evaluate it and work things out with you." Putting this addendum in writing formalizes both your and your students' responsibilities. Students know that if they are going to be late, they must provide a written explanation, and you have an obligation to the student to work with the situation, within reason. The flexibility of this approach gives students who are going to be late motivation to complete the assignment rather than simply not turning it in at all.

Finishing Versus Learning

Getting students to complete homework is just one part of a larger equation. We need to consider the difference between simply completing homework and actually learning from it. Techniques that involve pressure, coercion, threats, rewards, and punishments might result in some, but not all, students completing assignments, but I believe we need to aim for something higher—students learning from their assignments. In a few cases, simply completing work without learning might be a reasonable goal. These cases include students with special needs who have limited capacity for comprehension and those students who refuse to let us help them no matter what we try. In these cases, first try techniques that use minimum pressure, then proceed cautiously with other types of interventions. For the vast majority of students, however, I suggest the following learning-based interventions to aid in both completion of and learning from homework.

Some of these interventions involve working with parents to change conditions at home. We know that some parents are unable to help through no fault of their own, some parents are unwilling to help, and some seem willing to help initially but ultimately do not follow through. I provide suggestions for handling each of these situations.

Improve conditions for doing homework. When conditions at home are conducive, students are far more likely to do their homework. The following conditions provide for a maximally conducive environment for homework completion and learning. The more of these conditions parents can meet, the better:

- Set up a designated homework area, ideally a well-lit, comfortable space with a desk or table outside the flow of traffic.
- Allow minimal snacking. A glass of milk or juice might be all that's needed. Avoid sweets.
- Minimize distractions. Do not allow other family members in the area during homework time. For most children, the television will need to be turned off or out of sight and earshot. If friends call or visit, they should be told that their friend is not available and given another time when they can call or visit. Music is OK if the child works better when listening to his or her favorite songs.
- Set a regular time. A routine is helpful for starting and completing homework, but for many households, adhering to a regular schedule is not possible. In these cases, try for the same time on certain nights—for example, 6 p.m. every Monday and Wednesday and 7 p.m. every Tuesday, Thursday, and Friday.
- Require the student to sit at the work area for the amount of time estimated for completion of the assignment. For example, if the student has roughly an hour's worth of homework, he or she should sit in the designated homework area for an hour. Obviously, parents and teachers will need to communicate to make sure these time guidelines are clear.
- Parents need not insist that the child do any work. They need only make sure that he or she sits in the designated area with the relevant school materials and proper supplies. This strategy works on two levels. First, most children would rather do anything than nothing; even doing homework is better than boredom. Second, simply getting started presents a substantial obstacle to homework completion. If students know they have an hour

ahead of them with nothing to do but homework, starting begins to seem less impossible. And once they begin an assignment, they are likely to complete it, unless they don't understand the content or the directions.

These conditions maximize the odds that students will get in the habit of doing homework on a regular basis. For those students who do not have parental or guardian supervision to establish this pattern, consider setting up homework study groups with three or four students at a home with a volunteer parent who can establish maximally conducive conditions. Barring that, petition the school to establish homework study clubs after school or during the day with the help of willing teachers or volunteers. (This is an ideal opportunity to involve elderly community members, as discussed in Chapter 6.) Regardless of the setup, this approach works best when attendance is voluntary rather than mandatory.

Involve students. Let students design homework for the class. Divide the class into groups and let each group develop a homework assignment built around an established goal or lesson plan. Let students choose which assignment to do from the list generated. For example, if you are reading a book in class, ask students to come up with questions about the plot, characters, or writing style. For a math class, ask them to create equations that reflect the current class lesson. Give yourself veto power over any inappropriate assignment.

Be provocative. Ask for opinions about controversies. Local ones work best. For example, "Should another Wal-Mart or McDonald's open in your neighborhood? Why or why not?" Of course, broader issues can be included if they are relevant to the classroom lesson.

Encourage doing good for others. Develop projects that incorporate service to others. These can include helping the elderly, raising money for charity, or cleaning up parks or neighborhoods. For some, even helping family members might be a new experience. Students can report on how the experience of helping felt, the reaction of those being helped, and the results of the project.

Five Hopeful Principles

I suggest these five hopeful principles for increasing homework completion:

1. When assigning homework, treat students you perceive as lazy, disconnected, hopeless, or uncaring in the same way you would treat students with

learning or physical disabilities. Replace the negative labels that come to mind with ones that reflect compassion and are less denigrating. This reframing process will make your interactions with these students more positive and open your mind to a new way of thinking about the assignments you give and how you evaluate them.

2. You have nothing to lose with students who never do their assignments when you allow them to do fewer problems. The immediate goal is to get them to complete one problem. Once that is accomplished, you can worry about getting them to complete them all.

3. Talk to struggling students one-on-one. Encourage their continued effort despite their difficulties with the material. You might say, "I can see that getting through this content has been hard for you, but I hope you don't give up. Why not try tonight and see what happens?"

4. Let students choose an alternative way to show they understand the content or have mastered the skills that the homework is trying to teach: "Donny, if there is a better way for you to show me that you can answer this question, I'll let you give it a try. Tell me what you *will do* before the end of the day."

5. Offer an alternative means of expression: "Monique, if you want to show that you understand this fraction problem, you can draw a pizza or something similar that illustrates the same principle. Let me know what you decide to draw."

Reaching Those Students Who Absolutely Do Not Care

Of course, none of these strategies will have any effect if students simply do not care about school, learning, their future, or themselves. Truly hopeless students won't even try doing an assignment to discover how meaningful or enjoyable it might be. Pressure has little or no effect. Most teachers give up trying, because their attempts only result in failure. Here are some suggestions with the potential to turn things around:

• Try designing one or two questions aimed specifically at the target student. "Bill, you love rap (or heavy metal or hip-hop or . . .) music so much, can you tell me how fractions are related to the music's distinctive sound?"

• Operate with the understanding that some work completed is better than none. Ask a student to pick just one or two questions on an assignment sheet and answer only those.

- Warn the student in advance that he or she will be called on in class to answer a specific question: "Manny, here's a heads-up. Tomorrow, I'm going to call on you to answer question 6. I hope you will be ready." If necessary, provide the student with the answer to "jump-start" hope.
- Vary the previous example by telling the student to choose any question he or she wants and to tell you before class which one to call on him or her to answer.

These four strategies are designed to get unmotivated students to do at least something, with the hope of gradually increasing their motivation to respond. Don't give up the expectation for homework from a totally uninvolved student. Continue to call on the student at least once each day to answer a question when reviewing assignments. Ask the student privately on a regular basis what changes he or she will make to successfully complete assignments. Keep focused on the future rather than on punishment for past failures. Demonstrate that it is always possible for the student to succeed and that your expectations have not diminished.

11

The Relationship Between Behavior and Motivation

Separating motivation problems and behavior management problems can present a challenge for teachers. The two are often intertwined; unmotivated students frequently misbehave and students who misbehave frequently do not care about learning. Hence, it can be difficult to distinguish a motivational issue from a behavioral issue. Although the symptoms look the same, and often the causes are similar, the solutions can be very different. For example, if Edgar does not do his homework, is it because he is defiant, unable, or uninterested? Each scenario requires a different intervention. Fortunately, it is not always necessary to figure out which is which. Sometimes a motivational solution can have a positive effect on behavior and vice versa. The best answer, when in doubt, is to use a combination of strategies that focus on both behavior and motivation.

It is important to keep in mind that ineffective behavior solutions can kill motivation. If Edgar is forced to sit down when he defiantly refuses to, then he will most likely lose motivation for the remainder of the lesson. Urban youth are particularly susceptible to the escalation of behavioral problems into motivational problems because of their need for control and saving face, both essential characteristics of urban survival. Let's examine how using the motivational strategies described in this book can be applied to discipline problems.

Treat Students with Dignity

When we discipline with dignity, treating students with respect and understanding —in short, when we treat them the way we expect them to treat us—behavioral problems rarely turn into motivational ones. When we discipline students with dignity, we do the following:

- We listen to their side of the story.
- We give them a real voice in the way things are run in the classroom.
- We never treat them in a way that we would not want them to treat other people. My golden rule is, "Treat students the way you want them to treat others."
- We avoid sarcasm, labels, threats, bribes, and public humiliation.
- We allow them to save face.
- We use the "system" to solve their problems, not to bury them.
- We say, "Let's see what we can do" rather than "We can't do that!"
- We appreciate them without manipulation.

Ms. Margolis, a 5th grade teacher in Albuquerque, New Mexico, uses discipline with dignity. She never scolds, lectures, or humiliates her students. When she has a problem with a student, she explains why the student's actions or words bother her and asks to hear the student's side of the story. For example, Ms. Margolis might say to a student, "Juan, when you use words like that, I feel that you don't care about me. I hope that's not true. Can you tell me what you really want me to hear with different words?"

Debunk the "Bad-Versus-Stupid" Dichotomy

Most students would rather be labeled "bad" than stupid. Being bad is often portrayed as heroic in our culture. Think of the movies and television shows that portray the hero as a rebel, rule breaker, or deviant. Heroes may be rebellious, but they are never stupid. When students are labeled "stupid" or "poor achievers," they may stop trying and become rule breakers. By doing so, they can feel that they have made a choice to be unsuccessful, which allows them to maintain a feeling of control over their situation.

Devon struggled to read out loud. He mispronounced words and was very slow, leading his classmates to make fun of him. Soon, Devon began to throw his book at other students when it was his turn to read. He began swearing at the teacher and eventually had to be referred to the main office. He solved his problem of humiliation over his poor reading skills by being bad. A better solution would have been to let Devon read silently during class, along with any other students who preferred to do so, and read out loud privately with a teacher, paraprofessional, or student tutor. In this intersection of discipline and motivation, the remedy for rule violations is grounded in finding ways to increase motivation.

Avoid Power Struggles

Power struggles, when students and teachers fight for control of a situation, escalate quickly as the stakes and tension rise. Both parties believe that giving in will show weakness, make them lose face with the rest of the class, and compromise their values. Once a power struggle begins, regardless of who wins the battle—and it is usually the teacher—the student's motivation greatly diminishes.

Remember, a power struggle presents only three options: the teacher stops it, the student stops it, or it continues to escalate. For many urban youth, backing down is seen as weakness. Beyond humiliating the student in the classroom, this can have personal safety ramifications in that students who are perceived as weak may be seen as targets by bullies or gang members. It falls to us, then, to stop power struggles and to model how to do so without being perceived as weak. The best way to stop power struggles is to refuse to participate in them. The following are examples of how teachers can stop a power struggle before it begins:

- "I won't fight with you. Let's discuss this later."
- "I can see you feel strongly about this. Can you tell me why?"
- "We need a solution that makes both of us happy. Here's what I'm willing to do. What are you willing to do?"
- "I can see this means a lot to you. Take a few minutes to see if you can find a solution and I'll talk with you about it shortly."

Some teachers worry about backing off or allowing misbehavior to continue for even a short time, but these options seem preferable to getting into a battle than can only make things worse on both the motivation and the behavior fronts.

Offer Choices

Offering choices for the resolution of behavioral problems works in much the same way as providing choices for academic assignments. Both allow students to feel that they have some control over the outcome of the situation. As long as choices are not disguised threats, they preserve students' dignity and positively influence motivation. Students can be given choices about behavior, consequences for misbehavior, and strategies for solving problems:

- *Behavior decisions:* "You can do your work now, or if it makes more sense to you, after school with my help."
- *Consequences:* "In this classroom we don't insult others. You can write Ethan a letter of apology, do something nice for Ethan, or do something nice for the class."
- *Within consequences:* "You need to do something nice for Ethan. What would you like to do?"
- *Problem solving:* "I know you and Jules are unhappy with each other. Can you think of a way to improve your relationship, or would you like me to offer suggestions?"

When we give students choices as part of a plan to improve behavior, we increase their feelings of dignity and control, two powerful factors in increasing motivation.

Confront Cheating

When I was in college, I had a brilliant friend named Tallen. He was too smart to ever need to cheat, but he liked to see what he could get way with, and so he came up with one of the cleverest cheating schemes I have ever heard of. Before his final exam, he brought in two blue books. In the first one, he wrote, "Hi Ma, I just finished my psychology test and I think I did real well. Say hi to

Dad, and I'll see you in a few days when my finals are over." He handed that book in to his teacher and took the second, still-blank blue book home. He wrote his answers to the test questions in this second book using his notes and textbooks, and then mailed it home to his mother. He waited. His mother and teacher contacted him and each told him he had handed in the wrong book. He had his mother mail the book with the answers directly to the teacher. The teacher was fooled and gave him an *A*.

Just the opposite happened to me. I worked very hard to write a great paper on John Milton. My teacher, who, coincidentally, looked exactly like John Milton, wrote on the top, "This is a great paper. Too great for you. You must have cheated. You get a royal *F*." Needless to say, I hated both the real and the look-alike John Milton after that.

These two anecdotes demonstrate the problem with trying to address cheating: (1) How do you catch it, and (2) what if you are wrong? There is, of course, the old cheating chestnut of parents who do their children's work, but most cheating done today utilizes technology, which has made catching students at cheating a far more complex proposition. Students take pictures of tests with cell phones and pass them on to students in the next class, use cell phones to get answers during the test, and turn in papers purchased on the Internet. In short, it's a lot easier to cheat these days and a lot harder to be sure you are right when you suspect a student of cheating.

Further, both getting away with cheating and being falsely accused of cheating diminish motivation and make it harder on us. Students who get an *A* by cheating have little motivation to do any actual work, and students who are falsely accused may, understandably, feel persecuted and respond with a "Why bother?" attitude. Fortunately, solutions exist that allow us to detect and confront cheating without making possibly false accusations:

- Following the example of using hackers to improve computer security, ask a student you suspect of cheating to help you find classroom cheaters.
- Ask a student you suspect of cheating if he is willing to take the test again under tight observation. If he refuses, don't count the test. If he takes the test and does equally well, double the good grade. If he scores lower, double the poor grade. If the student refuses to take the "double down" opportunity, you know that he most likely cheated. And, further, he knows

that you know. Tell him that next time he might not have the option to refuse the double down.

• When I taught 7th grade, my class performed a play for other classes. As part of the assignment, I tasked students with making their own costumes. I gave the best grades to the worst costumes because I knew that those students truly had made them on their own. Conversely, I gave the worst grades to the professional-looking costumes because I knew those students' parents had made them.

• If you suspect that parents are doing their child's homework, call them in for a conference. Compliment them on caring so much about their children that they offer to help with homework while illustrating the line between helping and doing it for them. Explain to them how crossing that line cheats students of learning. Ideally, you should have this conversation with all parents.

• Cruise the classroom during tests, keeping an eye out for cell phone usage.

• Become familiar enough with the Internet to do searches for prewritten papers, and check any paper that seems overly well written.

• Tell a suspected student, "This paper is so good and beyond what most students your age can do that it almost made me think you cheated. Great job." Count the grade. You have just warned the student that you are watching her carefully without actually making a possibly false accusation.

• Give at least one assignment a month that allows cheating. Encourage creativity. Learn from what your students do and use it to catch real cheating in the future.

• Finally, never accuse a student of cheating if you are unsure that you are right.

Removal and Referrals

As we discussed in Chapter 6, removing students from the classroom kills motivation by sending the message that the student is unwelcome in class and that what we teach is not very important for that student to learn. But additional problems lie beneath the surface.

In the 1950s and early 1960s, one of television's most popular shows was *Father Knows Best,* which revolved around the Andersons, a typical suburban nuclear family. Whenever Bud, the teenage son, got in trouble, his mother would say, "Wait till your father gets home!" As the title of the show implied, Mother may have run the household, but Father was the true authority figure. Similarly, if a teacher sends a student to the office, he or she is essentially saying, "Wait until the principal finds out about this!" The name of the "show" becomes *Administrator Knows Best,* implicitly calling into question the teacher's authority and worth. The student eventually gets to leave the administrator's office, having promised to never again do whatever he was sent to the office for. Unfortunately, the one person who needs to hear that promise—the teacher—is left out of the process.

One possible alternative to referrals is for teachers to form teams of three or four. When one teacher needs a break from a student, he or she can send that student to a teammate's class rather than the office. Students rarely, if ever, bother the new class and sometimes even participate in class activities. This technique reduces the "Father Knows Best" syndrome, paperwork, student resentment, and loss of teacher control over the outcome of the problem.

If the teacher does opt to refer the student, he or she must accept certain outcomes. First, the teacher gives up all rights of control when he or she refers a student and must accept the administrator's handling of the situation. Second, the teacher must actively welcome the student back into the classroom regardless of any face-saving behavior on the part of the student. It is not realistic to expect the student to be publicly contrite. Lastly, the teacher needs to eventually solve the problem with the student, with the administrator's help if necessary.

Sometimes, of course, a student absolutely must be referred. Involvement in illegal activities—violence, drug use or distribution, or inappropriate sexual conduct, for example—requires an administrator's intervention.

Prevent Problems from Occurring

Preventing problems before they start is a sound motivational strategy, for obvious reasons. The following strategies either minimize behavior problems or prevent them from affecting motivation.

Maintain a physical presence in the room. Continually move around the room so that you are near every student during the lesson for at least a short time. Students need to feel you as well as see and hear you.

Establish social contracts with your class. A social contract is a list of values, rules, and consequences that define proper behavior deemed necessary for learning and teaching to occur (Curwin, Mendler, & Mendler, 2008). A value is necessarily broader than a rule because its purpose is to provide the reason behind the rule. An example of a value would be "We solve our problems peacefully," and a rule for students that might come from that value would be "If we have a disagreement that we cannot solve, we ask the teacher to help us find a solution."

Mike Krzyzewski, the successful coach of the Duke University basketball team, coached the 2008 U.S. Olympic team in China, a team composed of famous, rich, and highly successful players. In his book *The Gold Standard* (Krzyzewski & Spatola, 2009), he describes how, after forming the team, the players got together to define their collective values, a process that bonded them and established the mission, rules of behavior, and attitudes that carried them through the Olympics. Social contracts can provide the same sense of continuity and cohesion for students.

Social contracts generally work best when teachers identify the school or classroom values and then involve students in defining the rules. In most school districts, key values are established by the school board and are included, along with rules, in a policy manual.

Here are three values that make great starting points for developing rules and expectations for the classroom:

- Everyone who enters this room will learn.
- Everyone will be physically, mentally, and emotionally safe here.
- Everyone in this room will take responsibility for his or her behavior.

Once these values are established and understood, offer specific examples of related rules. Here are some examples:

Value: Everyone who enters this room will learn.

Rule: Do not talk when the teacher or another student is speaking.

Value: Everyone will be physically, mentally, and emotionally safe here.

Rule: Keep your hands and feet to yourself.

Value: Everyone in this room will take responsibility for his or her own behavior.

Rule: Accept a consequence for breaking rules without argument.

Notice that rules are stated in terms of behavior and values in terms of attitudes. Both are equally necessary for effective discipline and problem prevention.

Encourage students to fully participate in the contract by proposing specific rules. Allow for class discussion and seek consensus. Consider allowing your students to propose rules for you, as well. You might ask, "I'd like to know what you think I could or should do that will best help you learn. Come up with a rule or two that you would like to see me follow."

Make sure your expectations are clear from the start. Make sure your students understand what you expect from them with regard to procedures, performance standards, and treatment of others in the classroom. Part of doing this involves going over the established values, rules, and consequences. Explain what you mean by "fair is not equal." The more clarity students have about your expectations for them and the earlier they have it, the less likely they are to fail to meet them out of ignorance.

Set up a tutoring system. As we discussed earlier, students learn well from one another. With this in mind, set up a program that allows students who are proficient in a certain area to help those who are less proficient. Have each student make a small poster listing what he or she is good at in relation to the topics covered in class. Have them hang the posters on the wall in a designated "I can help" area. Teachers of younger students can help in the development of posters, or students can help one another make posters. Make either seeking help from or offering help to other students evidence of effort.

Set up a student complaint system. Let students know from the beginning that they have the right to complain, make classroom improvement suggestions, and tell you how they are feeling about the class, provided they do it in a respectful way, using appropriate language and intending to make things better.

Students can use various methods to report complaints in a constructive manner. Young children can use a "pass the teddy bear" technique, where the students form a circle and pass a teddy bear to anyone who wants to speak. For older children, a "gripe box" can be set up for signed or anonymous complaints, or students can get together with the teacher for open discussion about problems or concerns.

You do not have to accept any suggestion that makes you uncomfortable, but try to accommodate as many requests as possible within your comfort zone. Doing so can keep minor problems from developing into larger issues. Try to avoid reacting defensively to students who make complaints or suggestions. Focus on explaining your point of view without criticizing the legitimacy of the complaint. A possible response might be, "That problem makes sense to me, but here are some reasons why I can't let you talk whenever you want." Give your reasons and then continue, "How about taking a five-minute break every day after we do our lesson when you can talk to your friends?"

Find out what helps students learn. Early on in any course, ask your students what other teachers have done in the past that helped them succeed or, conversely, kept them from succeeding. Also ask what they did themselves that helped them succeed or not succeed. Hang up two posters in the room based on these answers, one marked "Here's what I will do" and the other marked "Here's what you will do."

Better Behavior via Motivation—and Vice Versa

Motivation and behavior are so intrinsically connected that parsing out the difference between motivation problems and behavioral problems is not always possible. This means that it can be difficult to figure out which type of problem to address. The good news is that often, it does not matter. Improving students' behavior will increase their motivation, and increasing students' motivation will improve their behavior. Either way, you'll be making a difference.

12

For the Administrator

Several years ago, my colleague Al Mendler and I developed a simulation that included four groups: administrators, students, teachers, and parents. Our goals were to show the relative power of each group in relation to the others; to discover effective versus ineffective negotiation strategies on the basis of each group's assessment of what it had to offer the others and what power it could generate; and to demonstrate that good administrators have many needs to meet and very little to gain for themselves. Each person put in a dollar, and each group had the opportunity to make money except for the administrator group. No one knew this except the administrators, who had the responsibility of deciding which groups received the money and how much each received. In the end, no matter how the money was distributed, everyone was angry with the administrators. We believed that this accurately reflected the frequently challenging life of administrators, one filled with great responsibility to satisfy others with little gain for themselves. It takes someone who loves children to do it well.

School administrators must please a number of groups, many of which are in conflict with one another. From teachers and parents to school boards and government agencies, the pressure to meet every group's needs is enormous. Ultimately, however, any policy enacted by administrators—whether related to curricula, testing, or behavior—must have at its core the goal of motivating children. If students don't want to learn, nothing else matters. Here are 10 suggestions derived from the chapters in this book that can help administrators achieve this goal.

Combat Cynicism

Cynicism can not only kill student motivation but also poison an entire school's culture. Administrators must actively fight against cynicism to get the best out of students and teachers. The following five strategies can help administrators maintain a hopeful, productive school environment:

- **Set a positive tone.** In staff meetings, emphasize that cynicism will not be tolerated. Explain your reasons why. Define the difference between cynicism (the loss of hope) and skepticism (refusing to accept ideas without critically examining them). Ask for suggestions from your staff on how to reduce or eliminate negativity in your school. Emphasize that no student can learn in a negative atmosphere and that cynicism destroys motivation. Be positive yourself when interacting with staff.

- **Organize a group of great motivators among your staff.** Organize a small group of your best teachers and assign them the task of developing strategies to combat cynicism. Let them know that this is one of your highest priorities and act on the strategies they develop as quickly as possible.

- **Meet with cynical teachers.** Arrange private meetings with teachers you have identified as negative. Ask them how the school year is going for them, what could be improved, and whether they are satisfied with their performance. Discuss ways in which these teachers can combat their cynicism. Be caring but firm in this and in all future discussions with them. Put them in charge of their own progress, but hold them accountable for their improvement.

- **Get marginal teachers involved.** Most schools have a group of teachers who are not yet cynical but might become so. Get these teachers involved in leadership roles and projects the same way you would include students who are only marginally interested in learning.

- **Immunize new staff against cynicism.** When hiring new staff and during their first year in your school, strongly and clearly emphasize your position on negativity. Stress how important it is to function as an active, positive role model for students and as a supportive colleague to the rest of the staff.

Support a Focus on Effort

When teachers are involved in motivational training, most agree that focusing on effort makes sense but complain that their administrators won't let them try it. Of course, some administrators are so blinded by the desire to get high test scores that they fail to see that effort is what creates the highest scores possible. But these ineffective administrators are rare. Far more common is a lack of communication between teachers and administrators, combined with the constant pressure on both to meet standards imposed by others.

Let your staff know how strongly you support strategies and techniques that focus on effort. Let them know that you understand that achievement is a result of effort, and that you will back up their endeavors to increase student effort.

In addition, communicate to your staff that what students bring to the teacher influences learning as much as what the teacher brings to the student. Just as firefighters cannot be held accountable for saving every structure that catches on fire, teachers cannot be expected to save every student. All they can do is their best. Tell your staff that you expect effort from them and that they will be judged on how hard they try to reach all students rather than on test results, which are beyond their control.

By recognizing effort from both staff and students, you will maximize your test results and reduce the negative influence of test pressure.

Support Innovation

Most good teachers continually try new things to motivate their students. Innovation is often stifled, however, by a combination of factors, including school procedure and policy, the belief that the best innovation must be research-based, and a fear of judgment from fellow teachers who prefer to maintain the status quo.

Of course, not all innovation is effective. Just because something is new doesn't necessarily make it better. But the only way to determine a new technique's effectiveness is to try it. School policy should encourage experimentation because that's how effective strategies come to the fore. Encourage teachers to try out new techniques, even if they sound odd. It's difficult to truly harm a student who already refuses to learn, so why not try something different? Set time aside at each staff meeting for teachers to share innovations. Make your school a learning laboratory where great ideas are discovered and shared.

Eliminate Curriculum Alignment

Efforts to homogenize the curriculum by aligning it with standards and scripting it so that all teachers are on the same page and every student receives the same instruction in the same format at the same time runs counter to the basic principles of creativity, individualization, motivation, and student-centered learning. It leads to treating teachers as curriculum managers rather than educators.

Individualize Standards

We need standards. They provide a measuring stick by which to ascertain progress. To be maximally effective as a measure and motivator, however, standards must be individualized. When standards are set too high, failure is inevitable for some students. Standards need to be high enough to have meaning, but if they are impossible for some students to reach, they violate the most basic principle of education: school is for all children.

Conversely, setting standards too low creates an artificial "finish line." Students are not encouraged to explore the limits of their abilities. If students are to maximize their potential, they must be challenged to perform at their highest level of effort.

It is not our responsibility to decide which students are qualified for college or the workforce, although we can help in that process. Our responsibility is to teach every student as much as we can while we have him or her in our schools.

Promote Student Performances

Having students perform in front of an audience—other classes, parents, or community members, for example—is a powerful motivator. Knowing that others will see their work increases students' desire to do a good job and thus increases their effort. Students can present plays, music recitals, science demonstrations, and advertisements like those discussed in Chapter 7.

All students can participate, although not all have to perform. Accommodate your students' varying interests and talents by having them work as writers, stagehands, set designers, ushers, invitation makers, or hosts and hostesses. Every school can easily have several performances per month, provided they are based on lesson content.

Create Opportunities to Help

"Helping opportunities" are a versatile tool for any teacher or administrator. They can be used as a welcoming technique, as a consequence, as a motivator, and as a way to incorporate altruism into the school culture. As an administrator, you can facilitate this process by making helping others an official part of school policy. These strategies will help you accomplish this:

- Set up student tutoring centers.
- Use the altruism consequence (Chapter 6) when students are referred to you.
- Create a policy that no student can be excluded from helping others due to bad behavior.
- Create partnerships with other schools and different grade levels with the goal of providing students with opportunities to tutor or mentor younger students.
- Catalog ways for students to help one another within your school, ranging from cafeteria duty, hall monitor duty, and playground supervision to tutoring, protecting students who are being bullied, and welcoming new students.
- Explain to parents the purpose and benefits of an altruistic school and get their support.

• Start small. Recruit a small group of teachers to begin incorporating helping opportunities into their rotation of motivational and behavior management strategies. If the trial run goes well, widen the program's scope.

• Develop a plan to deal with the logistics of implementing a formal helping program.

Minimize Inappropriate Rewards and Punishments

In Chapter 4, we looked at the dangers of using rewards as bribes and the futility of applying punishments to already punishment-satiated students. The following suggestions are aimed at helping you achieve a better balance of rewards and punishments versus appreciations and consequences:

• Base the honor roll, class rankings, and other honors on effort rather than achievement. Consider the truism, as stated by economist John Maynard Keyes, that "nothing corrupts society more than to disconnect effort and reward" (Keyes, quoted in Perlstein, 2009).

• Use referrals only as a last resort rather than as a primary punishment.

• Teach students the social skills that they haven't learned at home. No student should be penalized because of inadequate parental guidance.

• Eliminate programs of color-coded behavior designations, the renaissance program, or any other program based on "catching a child at being good."

• Remember that if a behavior modification or motivational program is truly working, students will adhere to the program's principles regardless of whether they are being watched. Any program that requires constant monitoring of students to ensure the desired outcome is most likely doomed to failure in the long run.

• Keep all interventions private. Do not make examples of students, either as positive or as negative role models.

• Discard the idea of "zero tolerance." Replace it with appropriate tolerance. Blanket application of a zero tolerance policy can have unintended, sometimes severe, consequences for both children and schools. We wouldn't want a child to have zero tolerance, so why promote it in our schools?

Appreciate Teacher Efforts to Motivate

To create a culture of motivation in your school, teachers need to know that you appreciate their efforts to reach unmotivated students. Appreciations for teachers, like those for students, are best done privately, but there are ways to acknowledge collective staff efforts without publicly singling out any one individual.

Consider holding a coffee-and-bagel party one or two mornings a month in appreciation of staff initiatives and successes. Send out thank-you notes to those teachers who have gone above and beyond to reach difficult children. Send a note home to selected students' parents informing them of their child's teacher's efforts.

Be a cheerleader, suggestion generator, sounding board, and gripe defuser. But keep in mind that the one thing you cannot be is a friend. Although it sounds harsh, you can't be a friend to all the teachers in your school, and being a friend to some of them can create personal conflicts, especially when making tough assignment choices. Friends don't criticize or make demands of one another, but you may have to do both in your capacity as an administrator. Maintain a friendly, professional attitude without crossing the line.

Welcome All Students

You can go a long way toward creating a culture of motivation by personally welcoming all students, especially the least motivated. If you cut down on referrals, you will have more time to assert a physical presence in your school, which is key for establishing rapport with students. Here are some welcoming strategies you can use on a regular basis, some every day:

- Greet students at the door at the beginning of school. Wish them a good day.
- Say goodbye to individual students at the close of the school day.
- Walk around the lunchroom and check in with as many tables as possible. Be sure to connect with "high-priority" students.
- Cruise the corridors between classes. Greet students by name.

- Drop in to every class for five minutes or so each week. Let students know you are around and that you are paying attention to them.
- Teach a class every now and then.
- Always listen to the student's side of the story, even if you know it's a fabrication, an excuse, or an attempt to shift blame. You don't have to agree as long as you really listen. Even when being duplicitous, students will sometimes unintentionally reveal a clue as to what is really going on.
- Encourage good communication between parents and teachers. Be a facilitator more than a problem solver.
- Be very slow to remove children from learning and extracurricular activities. Be very quick to teach them positive social skills.

Final Thoughts

Few understand the responsibilities, constituencies, and demands that administrators face daily. Every teacher, school board member, student, parent, community member, and government agency has an agenda, and these agendas rarely exist in concert with one another. Administrators are expected to somehow satisfy all of these varied agendas—a near impossibility. Given all the obstacles and challenges, I sometimes wonder why anyone would want this job. I find the answer every time I visit a school and see just how much administrators care about students and how hard they work to promote their well-being.

Conclusion: A Place Where Dreams Come True

In this book, I have purposely avoided looking at the "big picture," preferring instead to look at the things that all educators can do to foster motivation at the school and classroom levels. This is, after all, what we can control and therefore change. I now wish to pull the lens back a bit and share my overall vision for what urban schools can be.

Cleveland, Pittsburgh, Indianapolis, and Baltimore are cities, among many others, that had at one time decayed to the point of appearing irretrievably ugly to me. Now, thanks to urban rejuvenation programs, they have been largely restored and are, to my eye, reborn. It is time to do the same for our urban schools—not just the physical structures but also, and more importantly, the internal structures that promote learning. Here is my dream for what urban schools can become:

• Schools follow curricula that meet the needs of each child rather than forcing children into predetermined little boxes that may or may not have anything to do with their lives. No more alignment, mapping, or teaching to the test. No more one-size-fits-all instruction. Curricula are designed to accommodate needs we do not even know about yet, based on a world that our students will create.

- Every school has high standards for all students, attainable by all. No standards are so high that some students are predestined to fail. No standards are so easy that some students can pass without working or even learning. No students can pass without effort, and none can fail if they expend effort.
- All evaluation is diagnostic in nature, with the singular goal of helping students learn. Judging the worth of performance is a distant cousin to seeing improvement, especially if that judgment interferes with the learning process in any way. We no longer compare students with one another, labeling some winners and others losers.
- Rubrics, standards, curriculum alignment, IEPs, policies, rules, and systems are all geared toward achieving the only goal that matters: getting students to want to learn. Schools operate on the understanding that students will achieve only if they want to, and all the rubrics, standards, curriculum alignment, IEPs, policies, rules, and systems are totally useless if a child does not care about his or her own learning.
- There is sufficient time built into the day for physical education and play. Adequate time is allotted for the arts, including music, drama, visual arts, and creative writing. Teachers have time, too, for planning, observing, creating, and problem solving. Administrators have time to communicate effectively with staff and students without rushing through preplanned agendas.
- Homogeneous groupings are nonexistent until high school. Children mature at different rates, and learning varies too greatly to determine who can be labeled superior or average (Gladwell, 2008). These labels become self-fulfilling prophecies that prematurely determine a student's future. Students should have the opportunity to figure out their strengths and needs before the sorting process begins.
- Sports are for all students, not just the "good" athletes. Schools provide more outlets, athletic clubs, and leagues—both intramural and extramural—so that all who want to play can. I recently attended a Texas high school football game. It was exciting, in part, because the teams were playing at such a high skill level. At the end of the game, however, I felt sorrier for the winning quarterback than for the losing one. He was a senior, and I feared that his greatest moment in life might have been that win. No one should have the

best day of his life in high school. Schools can balance high performance and the excitement of athletics as a part of the school experience, not as the entire school experience.

• Finally, I dream that schools in the future operate on the four pillars of academic greatness:

1. School is for all students, not just the good ones.

2. Everyone who enters school will learn.

3. Our job as educators is not to decide who students will become, but to make them better at being who they already are.

4. Students do not come to school for us; we go to school for them.

Every child has a dream; some are squashed, some denied, some encouraged, and some realized. What if the goal of every school, carved in stone above its entrance, was to be "a place where dreams come true"?

Ten Books Worth Reading

Conscious Classroom Management: Unlocking the Secrets of Great Teaching, by Rick Smith. (2004). San Rafael, CA: Conscious Teaching Publications.

Smith reveals several useful strategies and methods that can improve the motivation of all children. This is one of the best books on classroom management I've read.

Different Brains, Different Learners: How to Reach the Hard to Reach, by Eric P. Jensen. (2000). Thousand Oaks, CA: Corwin Press.

One of the leaders in brain research and application, Jensen shows how to apply this knowledge to motivate and individualize lessons for learners who typically fail in traditional school settings.

Flow: The Psychology of Optimal Experience, by Mihaly Csikszentmihalyi. (1990). New York: Harper & Row.

In this classic book, Csikszentmihalyi examines how tasks can be made to motivate. His extensive research and brilliant conclusions have informed my work and helped me understand the underlying principles of effort.

Healing Racism in America: A Prescription for the Disease, by Nathan Rutstein. (1993). Springfield, MA: Whitcomb Publishers.

Rutstein takes on the tough issue of racism and finds viable solutions, offers commonsense suggestions, and demonstrates true commitment to resolving this devastating social ill.

Lessons from Exceptional School Leaders, by Mark F. Goldberg. (2001). Alexandria, VA: ASCD.

Goldberg clearly and intelligently shows administrators how to be real leaders. Implementing change takes more than desire and courage; it also takes skill. Goldberg demonstrates plenty of all three.

Outliers: The Story of Success, by Malcolm Gladwell. (2008). New York: Little, Brown.

Gladwell's book explores some of the misconceptions about success in ways that have direct application to the ways schools are formulated. His thesis offers a fresh look at achievement and motivation and how they can be enhanced.

Punished by Rewards: The Trouble with Gold Stars, Incentive Plans, A's, Praise, and Other Bribes, by Alfie Kohn. (1993). Boston: Houghton Mifflin.

Kohn explores the myths behind offering rewards for achievement and shows ways to teach without them. For those who still think bribing children is an effective educational strategy, this book is the antidote.

Reclaiming Youth at Risk: Our Hope for the Future, by Larry K. Brendtro, Martin Brokenleg, & Steve Van Bockern. (1990). Bloomington, IN: National Educational Service.

Full of insights, suggestions, and hope, this groundbreaking book examines both how we lose children and how we can get them back.

Today's Best Classroom Management Strategies: Paths to Positive Discipline, by C. M. Charles. (2008). Boston: Pearson Education.

Charles provides a complete and substantive explanation and analysis of the major models of behavioral theories and principles in use in education today. This book is particularly helpful for new teachers.

Transforming Classroom Grading, by Robert J. Marzano. (2000). Alexandria, VA: ASCD.

Marzano challenges us to make sense of the senseless way we evaluate student learning. He offers models, strategies, and insights that can make evaluation an integral part of the learning process rather than the destroyer of learning that it currently is.

Appendix A
Phonics Challenge Worksheet
2nd Grade

Directions: Identify the underlined vowel(s) in each word. Use the following key:

U = Short Vowel	—— = Long Vowel	R = R-controlled vowels
VT = Vowel Team	ME = Magic E	

bed ____   car ____   dream ____

green ____   window ____   newspaper ____

scissors ____   can ____   race ____ and ____

computer ____ and ____   blue ____   donut ____ and ____

pencil ____ and ____   near ____   yellow ____

watermelon ____ and ____   never ____ and ____

peanut butter ____ and ____ and ____   student ____ and ____

princess ____ and ____   baseball ____ and ____   soap ____

fact ____   principal ____ and ____   vacation ____ and ____

delicate ____ and ____   free ____   payback ____ and ____

magic ____ and ____   groan ____

A variety of fun learning games can be found online to teach the concepts illustrated in this challenge sheet. The following two offer free games for R-controlled vowels:

- http://www.sadlier-oxford.com/phonics/grade2_3/pg_142/begin_dia2.htm
- http://hill.troy.k12.mi.us/staff/bnewingham/myweb3/literacy_centers%20Final.htm

Submitted by Jeanette Gibbs, speech/language therapist, grades K–3, Whitfield Elementary School, West Lawn, Pennsylvania

Appendix B
Texture Drawing Worksheet
9th Grade

- Divide your paper into eight sections.
- Draw a heart in each section. (*Note for teachers: The hearts can be pre-printed on a piece of paper and photocopied.*)
- Apply the texture described below in each heart.
- Use the appropriate medium (the supply that is described—for example, regular pencil, pen, colored pencils).
- You will have 20 minutes to complete this task. Circle the tasks that you think you can complete in 20 minutes.

Heart #1. Color the heart solid with regular pencil.

Heart #2. Color the heart with a checkerboard design using a black marker.

Heart #3. Color the heart with a monochromatic blend of your choice using colored pencils. Example: Dark blue fading to light blue.

Heart #4. Shade the heart using 3D value shading to achieve a three-dimensional appearance.

Heart #5. Add shading to the heart with small pinpoint dots (stippling). Use a thin black marker.

Heart #6. Add textured cross-hatching lines in and outside of the heart to make it look prickly like a cactus. Use a thin black marker or a regular pencil.

Heart #7. Illustrate the heart to make it appear as if it is melting. Use your choice of medium to achieve realistic shading.

Heart #8. Shade the heart to appear as if it is made out of glass. Use a ballpoint pen—blue or black.

Submitted by Lorijean Wallence, art teacher, Wilson Central Junior High School, West Lawn, Pennsylvania

Appendix C
Landscape Installation Challenge Worksheet
High School–Level Mathematics Application

Name: _____

Date: _____

1. Find the area of a garden that measures 100 feet x 50 feet.

2. If a 10-6-4 fertilizer is applied to this area (using the recommended spreader setting), how many bags are required and of what size? Choose the product that will be most cost-effective for the consumer.

   5,000 square feet $9.99
   10,000 square feet $14.99
   15,000 square feet $19.99

3. A 3-inch mulch border is required for that area. How many cubic yards of shredded bark is needed to cover that area to a depth of 3 inches? (Use an estimated calculation if you have no calculator.)

4. Mulch is priced at $25/cubic yard. What is the cost?

5. If 6-foot spruce trees are planted along the perimeter, 25 feet on center, how many of these evergreens should be ordered for the job?

6. Six-foot spruce trees are priced at $50.00. What is the cost to the landscaper for the plant material?

7. The landscaper needs to make a profit of 50 percent. What should she charge the homeowner?

8. How many bricks are required to cover a triangular area that measures 30 feet at the base and 20 feet at the height (4.5 bricks cover 1 square foot)?

9. This project requires a 4-inch mason sand base. How many tons of sand should be ordered?

10. A circular bed, intended for groundcover, measures 20 feet in diameter. Pachysandra is packaged in flats of 50 plants. One flat covers 25 square feet. How many flats of pachysandra are required to cover this area?

Submitted by Peg Tinder, horticulture teacher, Owen J. Roberts High School, Pottstown, Pennsylvania

Appendix D
Measurement Challenge Worksheet
High School–Level Family and Consumer Science Course
in Food Preparation

Dash, a few grains = _____ teaspoon(s)

3 teaspoons = _____ tablespoon(s)

16 tablespoons = _____ cup(s)

8 tablespoons = _____ cup(s)

4 tablespoons = _____ cup(s)

2 cups = _____ pint(s)

2 pints = _____ quart(s)

4 quarts = _____ gallon(s)

16 ounces = _____ pound(s)

8 fluid ounces = _____ cup(s)

4 fluid ounces = _____ cup(s)

2 fluid ounces = _____ cup(s)

1 fluid ounce = _____ cup(s) or _____ tablespoon(s)

1 pound butter/margarine = _____ cup(s) or _____ stick(s)

1 stick butter/margarine = _____ cup(s)

Answer Key

Dash, a few grains = less than 1/8 teaspoon

3 teaspoons = 1 tablespoon

16 tablespoons = 1 cup

8 tablespoons = 1/2 cup

4 tablespoon = 1/4 cup

2 cups = 1 pint

2 pints = 1 quart

4 quarts = 1 gallon

16 ounces = 1 pound

8 fluid ounces = 1 cup

4 fluid ounces = 1/2 cup

2 fluid ounces = 1/4 cup

1 fluid ounce = 1/8 cup or 2 tablespoons

1 pound butter/margarine = 2 cups or 4 sticks

1 stick butter/margarine = 1/2 cup

Submitted by Jocelyn Moyer, Wilson High School, West Lawn, Pennsylvania

Appendix E
Pre-Algebra Equations Challenge Worksheet
Upper-Elementary Level

1. $58 + 12 =$
2. $73 - 14 =$
3. $11 \times 11 =$
4. $156 / 4 =$
5. $45 + ? = 77$
6. $? - 22 = 33$
7. $a + 14 = 37$
8. $3c = 51$
9. $\dfrac{x}{14} = 3$
10. $3a + 12 = 63$
11. $\dfrac{16 - b}{2} = 4$

Submitted by Jaime Garman, East Vincent Elementary School, Spring City, Pennsylvania

Appendix F
Math Challenge Worksheet
6th Grade

Today's Magic Number: 192

What number is 100 more?   _____

What number is 100 less?   _____

What number is 1/2 of this number?   _____

What number is 1/4 of this number?   _____

What is this number plus your age?   _____

What is this number plus 1,000?   _____

How many hours and minutes would this be?   _____

If this were quarts, how many gallons of liquid would this be?   _____

If this were the temperature in Fahrenheit, would it be cold,
    hot, or warm?   _____

If this were inches, how many feet would this be?   _____

Appendix G
Social Studies Challenge Worksheet
Grades 9–12

Put these in order, earliest to latest:

1. 325 B.C.E.   2. 1940   3. 1865   4. 4 B.C.E.   5. 1961

Put these in the order they held the office of President:

1. Obama   2. Jefferson   3. Washington   4. Lincoln   5. FDR

Put these in order, lowest to highest:

1. Hills   2. Plateau   3. Sea level   4. Mountains   5. Plains

Match the items in row one with the items in row two.

1. Executive 2. Legislative 3. Judiciary   4. World government 5. World court

1. U.N.   2. The Hague 3. President 4. Congress   5. Supreme Court

Put in order, earliest to latest:

1. Free enterprise   2. Socialism   3. Bartering   4. Communism
5. Command economy

Submitted by Michael W. Chorazy, Juvenile Detention Center, Delaware County, Pennsylvania

Bibliography

Anno, M. (1977). *Anno's journey.* New York: Putnam Juvenile.

Appelbaum, M. (2008). *How to handle the hard-to-handle student, k–5.* Thousand Oaks, CA: Corwin Press.

Armstrong, T. (1987). *In their own way.* Los Angeles: Jeremy Tarcher.

Armstrong, T. (1998). *Awakening genius.* Alexandria, VA: ASCD.

Atkinson, D. A., & Juntunen, C. L. (1994). School counselors and school psychologists as school-home-community liaisons in ethnically diverse schools. In P. Pedersen & J. C. Carey (Eds.), *Multicultural counseling in schools: A practical handbook* (pp. 103–119). Needham Heights, MA: Allyn and Bacon.

Bagley, W. C. (1907). *Classroom management.* Norwood, MA: MacMillan.

Barros, R., Silver, E., & Stein, R. (2009, February). School recess and group classroom behavior. *Pediatrics, 123*(2), 431–436.

Beane, J. (2005). *A reason to teach.* Portsmouth, NH: Heinemann.

Bennett, S., & Kalish, N. (2006). *The case against homework: How homework is hurting our children and what we can do about it.* New York: Three Rivers Press.

Betances, S. (1998). *Ten steps to the head of the class.* Chicago: New Century Forum.

B'Hahn, C. (2002). *Mourning has broken: Learning from the wisdom of adversity.* Bath, UK: Crucible Publishers.

Blase, J., & Kirby, P. (2000). *Bringing out the best in teachers: What effective principals do.* Thousand Oaks, CA. Corwin Press.

Borba, M., & Borba, C. (1982). *Self-esteem: A classroom affair: 101 ways to help children like themselves.* San Francisco: Harper and Row.

Brendtro, L. K., Brokenleg, M., & Van Bockern, S. (1990). *Reclaiming youth at risk: Our hope for the future.* Bloomington, IN: National Educational Service.

Brendtro, L. K., Ness, A. E., & Mitchell, M. (2001). *No disposable kids.* Longmont, CO: Sopris West.

Brooks, R. (1991). *The self-esteem teacher: Seeds of self-esteem.* Circle Pines, MN: American Guidance Service.

Brown, E. (2003). Freedom for some, discipline for "others": The structure of inequality in education. In K. Saltman & D. Gabbard (Eds.), *Education as enforcement: The militarization and corporatization of schools.* New York: Routledge Falmer Press.

Campbell, L., & Campbell, B. (1999). *Multiple intelligences and student achievement.* Alexandria, VA: ASCD.

Carr, J., & Harris, D. (2001). *Succeeding with standards.* Alexandria, VA: ASCD.

Castilla, R. (2001). *Being down: Challenging violence in urban schools.* New York: Teachers College Press.

Charles, C. M. (2005). *Building classroom discipline* (8th ed.). Boston: Pearson Publishing.

Charles, C. M. (2008). *Today's best classroom management strategies: Paths to positive discipline.* Boston: Pearson Education.

Check, J. (2006). *Politics, language, and culture: A critical look at urban school reform.* Santa Barbara, CA: Greenwood Publishing Group.

Ciaccio, J. (2004). *Totally positive teaching.* Alexandria, VA: ASCD.

Committee for Children. (2002). *Second Step: A violence prevention curriculum, preschool/kindergarten.* Seattle, WA: Author.

Creemers, B. P. M., & Reezigt, G. J. (2005). Linking school effectiveness and school improvement: The background and outline of the project. *School Effectiveness and School Improvement, 16*(4), 359–371.

Crow, K., & Ward-Lonergan, J. (2002). *An analysis of personal event narratives produced by school-age children.* Paper presented at the annual meeting of the Council for Exceptional Children, New York.

Csikszentmihalyi, M. (1990). *Flow: The psychology of optimal experience.* New York: Harper & Row.

Curwin, R. (1992). *Rediscovering hope: Our greatest teaching strategy.* Bloomington, IN: National Educational Service.

Curwin, R. (1993, November). The healing power of altruism. *Educational Leadership, 51*(3), 36–39.

Curwin, R. (2002, March). Finding jewels in the rubble. *Educational Leadership, 59*(6), 80–83.

Curwin, R. (2003). *Making good choices.* Thousand Oaks, CA: Corwin Press.

Curwin, R. (2006). *Motivating students left behind: Practical strategies for reaching and teaching your most difficult students.* Rochester, NY: Discipline Associates.

Curwin, R., & Mendler, A. (1993, Fall). Classroom discipline without cultural bias. *School Safety*, 24–26.

Curwin, R., & Mendler, A. (1999, October). Zero tolerance for zero tolerance. *Phi Delta Kappan, 81*(2), 119–120.

Curwin, R., Mendler, A., & Mendler, B. (2008). *Discipline with dignity: New problems, new solutions* (3rd ed.). Alexandria, VA: ASCD.

Designs for Change. (2005, September 21). 144 Chicago inner city elementary schools serving nearly 100,000 students show 15 years of substantial and sustained achievement gains [Press release]. Retrieved October 7, 2009, from www.designsforchange.org/pdfs/ BP_pr_092105.pdf

DeVoe, J. F., Peter, K., Kaufman, P., Miller, A., Noonan, M., Snyder, T. D., et al. (2004). *Indicators of school crime and safety: 2004.* (NCES 2005–002/NCJ 205290). Washington, DC: National Center for Education Statistics. Retrieved October 7, 2009, from http://nces. ed.gov/pubs2005/crime_safe04/index.asp

Dohrmann, G. (2008, June 30). How dreams die. *Sports Illustrated.*

Driekers, R. (1964). *Children: The challenge.* New York: Hawthorn Books.

Erskine-Cullen, E., & Sinclair, A. (1996, March 25). Preparing teachers for urban schools: A view from the field. *Canadian Journal of Educational Administration and Policy, 6.*

Ferguson, A. (2000). *Bad boys.* Ann Arbor, MI: University of Michigan Press.

Gardner, H. (1983). *Frames of mind: The theory of multiple intelligences.* New York: BasicBooks.

Gardner, H. (1999). *The disciplined mind: Beyond facts and standardized tests, the K–12 education that every child deserves.* New York: Simon and Schuster.

Gladwell, M. (2008). *Outliers: The story of success.* New York: Little, Brown.

Goldberg, M. (2001). *Lessons from exceptional school leaders.* Alexandria, VA: ASCD.

Goldstein, A. (1999). *Teaching prosocial competencies.* Champaign, IL: Research Press.

Gonzalez, T. (2008, September 1). Know yr cell-phone messaging limits b4 U get caught @ school. *The Star Tribune* (Minneapolis). Retrieved October 7, 2009, from www.startribune. com/lifestyle/27726869.html

Gordon, R., Della Piana, L., & Keleher, T. (2001a). Zero tolerance: A basic racial report card. In W. Ayers, B. Dohrn, & R. Ayers (Eds.), *Zero tolerance.* New York: The New Press.

Gordon, R., Della Piana, L., & Keleher, T. (2001b). *Facing the consequences: An examination of racial discrimination in U.S. public schools.* Oakland, CA: Applied Research Center.

Greene, J. P., & Forster, G. (2004, January). *Sex, drugs, and delinquency in urban and suburban public schools, 4.* New York: Manhattan Institute for Policy Research.

Grunbaum, J. A., Kann, L., Kinchen, S., Ross, J., Hawkins, J., Lowry, R., et al. (2004, May 21). Youth risk behavior surveillance—United States, 2003. *MMWR Surveillance Summaries, 53*(2), 1–96.

Hamilton, B. E., Martin, J. A., & Ventura, S. J. (2006). Births: Preliminary data for 2005. *National Vital Statistics Reports, 55*(11). Hyattsville, MD: National Center for Health Statistics.

Harlow, C. W. (2003, January). *Special report: Education and correctional populations.* Washington, DC: Bureau of Justice Statistics, U.S. Department of Justice. Retrieved December 9, 2009, from http://bjs.ojp.usdoj.gov/content/pub/pdf/ecp.pdf

Harmon, M. (1974). *Teaching is.* Chicago: Science Research Associates.

Henley, M. (2003). *Teaching self-control.* Bloomington, IN: Solution Tree.

Hurren, L. (2006). The effects of principals' humor on teachers' job satisfaction. *Educational Studies, 2*(4), 373–385.

Hursh, D., & Ross, E. W. (2000). *Democratic social education: Social studies for social change.* New York: Falmer Press.

Interacting with and petting animals creates a hormonal response in humans that can help fight depression. (2004, May 14). *The Medical News*. Retrieved October 7, 2009, from www. news-medical.net/news/2004/05/14/1552.aspx

Jensen, E. (2000). *Different brains, different learners: How to reach the hard to reach*. Thousand Oaks, CA: Corwin Press.

Johnson, T., Boyden, J., & Pittz, W. (Eds.). (2001). *Racial profiling and punishment in U.S. public schools: How zero tolerance and high stakes testing subvert academic excellence and racial equity*. Oakland, CA: Applied Research Center.

Keith, S., & Martin, M. (2005). Cyber-bullying: Creating a culture of respect in a cyber world. *Reclaiming Children and Youth, 13*(4), 224.

Kerman, S., Kimball, T., & Martin, M. (1980). *Teacher expectations and student achievement*. Bloomington, IN: Phi Delta Kappa.

Kohn, A. (1990). *The brighter side of human nature: Altruism and empathy in everyday life*. New York: BasicBooks.

Kohn, A. (1993). *Punished by rewards: The trouble with gold stars, incentive plans, A's, praise, and other bribes*. Boston: Houghton Mifflin.

Krzyzewski, M., & Spatola, J. (2009). *The gold standard: Building a world-class team*. New York: Hachette Book Group.

Langrehr, J. (2001). *Teaching our children to think*. Bloomington, IN: National Educational Service.

Larsen, E. (2003). *Violence in U.S. public schools: A summary of findings*. Washington, DC: Institute of Education Sciences. (ERIC Document Reproduction Service No. 0889-8049)

Laub, J. H., & Lauritsen, J. L. (1998). The interdependence of school violence with neighborhood and family conditions. In D. Elliott, B. Hamburg, & K. Williams (Eds.), *Violence in American schools* (pp. 127–158). Cambridge, UK: Cambridge University Press.

Lenhart, A. (2009, August). *Teens and mobile phones over the past five years: Pew Internet looks back*. Washington, DC: Pew Internet & American Life Project.

Lippman, L., Burns, S., & McArthur, E. (1996). *Urban schools: The challenge of location and poverty*. Washington, DC: National Center for Education Statistics.

Loomans, D., & Kolberg, K. (2002). *The laughing classroom*. Novato, CA: H. J. Kramer/New World Library.

Losen, D., & Edley, C. (2001). The role of law in policing abusive disciplinary practices: Why school discipline is a civil rights issue. In W. Ayers, B. Dohrn, & R. Ayers (Eds.), *Zero tolerance*. New York: The New Press.

Luks, A. (1988, October). Helper's high: Volunteering makes people feel good, physically and emotionally. *Psychology Today*, 39–42.

Lundberg, E., & Thurston, C. M. (2002). *If they're laughing, they just might be listening: Ideas for using humor effectively in the classroom*. Fort Collins, CO: Cottonwood Press.

Lundin, S. C., Christensen, J., & Paul, H. (2002). *Fish tales*. New York: Hyperion.

Marzano, R. (2000). *Transforming classroom grading*. Alexandria, VA: ASCD.

Marzano, R. (2003). *What works in schools: Translating research into action*. Alexandria, VA: ASCD.

Marzano, R. J., & Marzano, J. S. (2003). The key to classroom management. *Educational Leadership, 61*(1), 6–18.

Meichenbaum, D. (1977). *Cognitive behavior modification*. New York: Plenum Press.

Mendler, A. (1997). *Power struggles.* Rochester, NY: Discipline Associates.

Mendler, A. (2000). *Motivating students who don't care*. Bloomington, IN: Solution Tree.

Mendler, A. (2001). *Connecting with students*. Alexandria, VA: ASCD.

Mendler, A. (2006). *Handling difficult parents*. Rochester, NY: Discipline Associates.

Mendler, A., & Curwin, R. (1999). *Discipline with dignity for challenging youth*. Bloomington, IN: Solution Tree.

Mendler, B., Curwin, R., & Mendler, A. (2008). *Strategies for successful classroom management*. Thousand Oaks, CA: Corwin Press.

Mlodinow, L. (2008). *The drunkard's walk: How randomness rules our lives*. New York: Pantheon Books.

Molnar, A., & Linquist, B. (1990). *Changing problem behavior in schools*. San Francisco: Jossey-Bass.

Moscowitz, F., & Hayman J. L. (1974). Interaction patterns of first year, typical, and "best" teachers in inner-city schools. *Journal of Educational Research, 67,* 224–230.

MTA Cooperative Group. (2004). National Institute of Mental Health multi-modal treatment study of ADHD follow-up: 24-month outcomes of treatment strategies for attention-deficit/hyperactivity disorder. *Pediatrics, 113,* 754–761.

Oliver, K. (2002). *Understanding your child's temperament*. The Ohio State University Extension, Family and Consumer Sciences. Retrieved October 7, 2009, from http://ohioline.osu.edu/flm02/FS05.html

Perlstein, R. (2009, March 30). Our American common sense. *Newsweek*.

Pool, C. R. (1997, May). Up with emotional health. *Educational Leadership, 52*(8), 12–14.

Postlethwaite, T. N., & Ross, K. N. (1992). *Effective schools in reading: Educations for educational planners*. Amsterdam: International Association for the Evaluation of Educational Achievement.

Richards, E. (2008, September 22). Stand-up desks provide a firm footing for fidgety students: Teachers report improved focus, behavior. *The Journal Sentinel* (Milwaukee, WI).

Rogers, S. (1999). *Teaching tips*. Evergreen, CO: Peak Learning Systems.

Rutstein, N. (1993). *Healing racism in America: A prescription for the disease*. Springfield, MA: Whitcomb Publishers.

Sigle-Rushton, W., & McLanahan, S. (2002). The living arrangements of new unmarried mothers. *Demography, 39*(3), 415–433.

Silver, H., Strong, R., & Perini, M. (2000). *So each may learn*. Alexandria, VA: ASCD.

Skiba, R., & Leone, P. (2001). Zero tolerance and school security measures: A failed experiment. In T. Johnson, J. Boyden, & W. Pittz (Eds.), *Racial profiling and punishment in U.S. public schools: How zero tolerance and high stakes testing subvert academic excellence and racial equity*. Oakland, CA: Applied Research Center.

Skiba, R., Michael, R., Nardo, C., & Peterson, R. (2002, December). The color of discipline: Sources of racial and gender disproportionality in school punishment. *The Urban Review, 34*(4), 317–342.

Smith, R. (2004). *Conscious classroom management: Unlocking the secrets of great teaching*. San Rafael, CA: Conscious Teaching Publications.

Stein, B. D., Jaycox, L. H., Kataoka, S. H., Wong, M., Tu, W., Elliott, M. N., et al. (2003). A mental health intervention for schoolchildren exposed to violence: A randomized controlled trial. *Journal of the American Medical Association, 290*(5), 603–611.

Stronge, J. H. (2002). *Qualities of effective teachers.* Alexandria, VA: ASCD.

Taub, J. (2002). Evaluation of the Second Step Violence Prevention Program at a rural elementary school. *School Psychology Review, 31*(2), 186–200.

Thomas-El, S., & Murphey, C. (2003). *I choose to stay: A black teacher refuses to desert the inner city.* New York: Dafina Books.

Toppo, G. (2006, June 20). Big-city schools struggle with graduation rates. *USA Today.* Retrieved November 25, 2009, from www.usatoday.com/news/education/2006-06-20-dropout-rates_x.htm

Truss, L. (2006). *Eats, shoots & leaves: The zero tolerance approach to punctuation.* New York: Gotham.

U.S. Department of Health, Education and Welfare. (1978). *Violent schools—safe schools. The safe school study report to the Congress.* (ERIC Document Reproduction Service No. ED 149 464)

Van de Grift, W. J. C. M., & Houtveen, A. A. M. (2006). Underperformance in primary schools. *School Effectiveness and School Improvement, 17*(3), 255–273.

Vavrus, F., & Cole, K. (2002, June). "I didn't do nothin'": The discursive construction of school suspension. *The Urban Review, 34*(2), 87–111.

Wald, J., & Losen, D. (Eds.). (2004a). *Deconstructing the school-to-prison pipeline: New directions for youth development.* Hoboken, NJ: Jossey-Bass.

Wald, J., & Losen, D. (2004b). *Defining and redirecting a school-to-prison pipeline.* Paper presented at the 2004 Midwest Conference on the Dropout Crisis: Assessing the Problem and Confronting the Challenge, Civil Rights Project at Harvard University, Cambridge, MA.

Wang, M. C., Haertel, G. D., & Walberg, H. J. (1997). Fostering educational resilience in inner-city schools. *Children and Youth, 7,* 119–140.

Weiner, B. (1974). *Achievement motivation and attribution theory.* Morristown, NJ: General Learning Press.

Wendt, M. (2002, Fall). Can exercise replace medication as a treatment for ADHD? *Healing Magazine,* 78.

Western, B., Pettit, B., & Guetzkow, J. (2002). Black economic progress in the era of mass imprisonment. In M. Mauer & M. Chesney-Lind (Eds.), *Invisible punishment: The collateral consequences of mass imprisonment* (pp. 165–180). New York: The New Press.

White, R., & Lippitt, R. (1960). Leader behavior and member reaction in three "social climates." In D. Cartwright & A. Zander (Eds.), *Group dynamics: Research and theory* (2nd ed.). New York: Row Peterson and Company.

Wong, H. K., & Wong, R. T. (1998). *The first days of school.* Mountain View, CA: Harry Wong Publications.

Index

About the Author

Dr. Richard L. Curwin is an author, trainer, speaker, and experienced education practitioner who has worked with teachers, administrators, and parents throughout the United States, Canada, Europe, Asia, South America, and the Middle East. His works explore issues of student discipline, motivation, and behavior and classroom management.

Having served as a 7th grade educator, a teacher of emotionally disturbed children, and a college professor, Dr. Curwin has a breadth of experience in the classroom. The behavior management strategies and philosophies he shares with educators have worked for him.

Curwin and Dr. Allen N. Mendler founded Discipline Associates and created the Discipline with Dignity program. Dr. Curwin coauthored *Discipline with Dignity for Challenging Youth* and *As Tough as Necessary: Countering Violence, Aggression, and Hostility in Our Schools*. He is also the author of *Making Good Choices* and *Motivating Students Left Behind*. Dr. Curwin's latest video set, *The Four Keys to Effective Classroom and Behavior Management,* which he developed with Dr. Mendler, won the 2007 Association of Educational Publishers Distinguished Achievement Award in the School/Class Management, Technology category. The third edition of *Discipline with Dignity: New Challenges, New Solutions* is an ASCD bestseller. He can be reached at richardcurwin@gmail.com.

Related ASCD Resources: Motivating Students in Urban Schools

At the time of publication, the following ASCD resources were available (ASCD stock numbers appear in parentheses). For up-to-date information about ASCD resources, go to www.ascd.org.

Multimedia

Making School Improvement Happen with What Works in Schools: An ASCD Action Tool Set by John L. Brown (#705055)

Online Courses

Visit the ASCD Web site (www.ascd.org) for the following professional development opportunities:
Understanding Student Motivation (#PD09OC76)
Understanding Student Motivation Challenges (#PD09OC77)

Print Products

Activating the Desire to Learn by Bob Sullo (#107009)

The Big Picture: Education Is Everyone's Business by Dennis Littky and Samantha Grabelle (#104438)

Closing the Achievement Gap: A Vision for Changing Beliefs and Practices (2nd edition) by Belinda Williams (#102010)

Discipline with Dignity, 3rd Edition: New Challenges, New Solutions by Richard L. Curwin, Allen N. Mendler, and Brian D. Mendler (#108036)

Educating Everybody's Children: Diverse Teaching Strategies for Diverse Learners (revised and expanded 2nd edition) by Robert W. Cole (Ed.) (#107003)

Educational Leadership, March 2008: Reaching the Reluctant Learner (#108025)

Inspiring Active Learning: A Complete Handbook for Today's Teachers (expanded 2nd edition) by Merrill Harmin and Melanie Toth (#103113)

Managing Diverse Classrooms: How to Build on Students' Cultural Strengths by Carrie Rothstein-Fisch and Elise Trumbull (#107014)

Mobilizing the Community to Help Students Succeed by Hugh B. Price (#107055)

The Motivated Student: Unlocking the Enthusiasm for Learning by Bob Sullo (#109028)

Motivating Black Males to Achieve in School and in Life by Baruti K. Kafele (#109013)

Motivating Students and Teachers in an Era of Standards by Richard Sagor (#103009)

Teachers as Classroom Coaches: How to Motivate Students Across the Content Areas by Andi Stix and Frank Hrbek (#106031)

Video and DVD

Educating Everybody's Children (one 70-minute DVD) (#600228)

Motivation: The Key to Success in Teaching and Learning (one 100-minute DVD with a Facilitator's Guide) (#603344)

A Visit to a Motivated Classroom (one 35-minute DVD with a comprehensive Viewer's Guide) (#603384)

WHOLE CHILD The Whole Child Initiative helps schools and communities create learning environments that allow students to be healthy, safe, engaged, supported, and challenged. To learn more about other books and resources that relate to the whole child, visit www.wholechildeducation.org.

For more information, visit us on the World Wide Web (www.ascd.org); send an e-mail message to member@ascd.org; call the ASCD Service Center (800-933-ASCD or 703-578-9600, then press 2); send a fax to 703-575-5400; or write to Information Services, ASCD, 1703 N. Beauregard St., Alexandria, VA 22311-1714 USA.